daybook, *n.* a book in which the events of the day are recorded; *specif.* a journal or diary

DAYBOOK
of Critical Reading and Writing

CONSULTING AUTHORS

FRAN CLAGGETT

LOUANN REID

RUTH VINZ

Great Source Education Group
a Houghton Mifflin Company
Wilmington, Massachusetts

www.greatsource.com

The Consulting Authors

Fran Claggett, currently an educational consultant for schools throughout the country and teacher at Sonoma State University, taught high school English for more than thirty years. She is author of several books, including *Drawing Your Own Conclusions: Graphic Strategies for Reading, Writing, and Thinking* (1992) and *A Measure of Success* (1996).

Louann Reid taught junior and senior high school English, speech, and drama for nineteen years and currently teaches courses for future English teachers at Colorado State University. Author of numerous articles and chapters, her first books were *Learning the Landscape* and *Recasting the Text* with Fran Claggett and Ruth Vinz (1996).

Ruth Vinz, currently a professor and director of English education at Teachers College, Columbia University, taught in secondary schools for twenty-three years. She is author of several books and numerous articles that discuss teaching and learning in the English classroom as well as a frequent presenter, consultant, and co-teacher in schools throughout the country.

Printed in the United States of America

International Standard Book Number: 0-669-46444-9

6 7 8 9 10 - RRDW - 04 03 02 01

Focus/Strategy	Lesson	Author/Literature

TABLE OF CONTENTS

ANGLES OF LITERACY

3

4

5

7

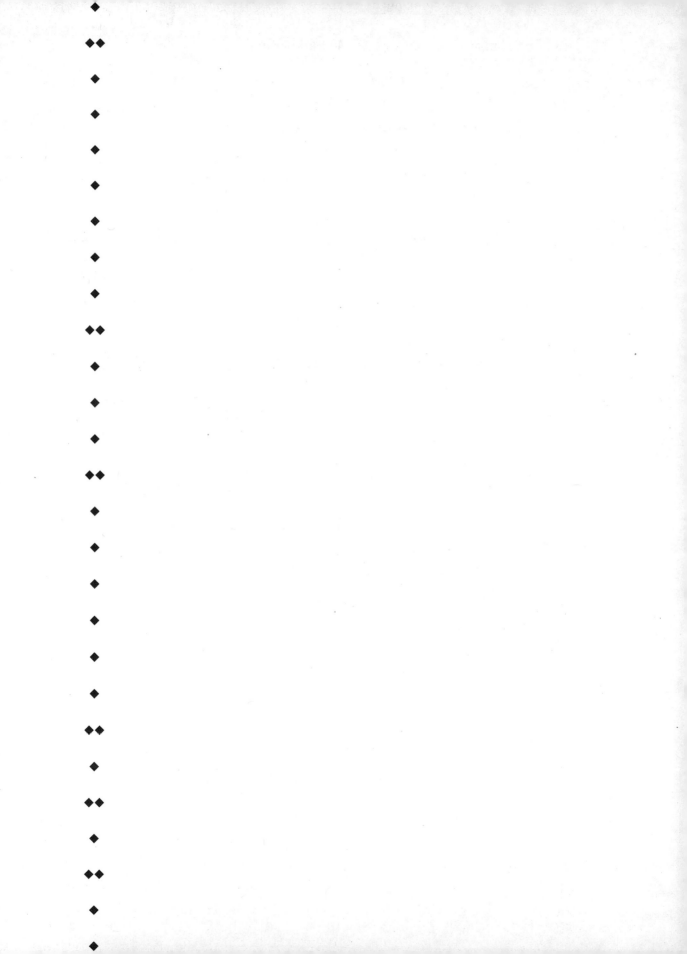

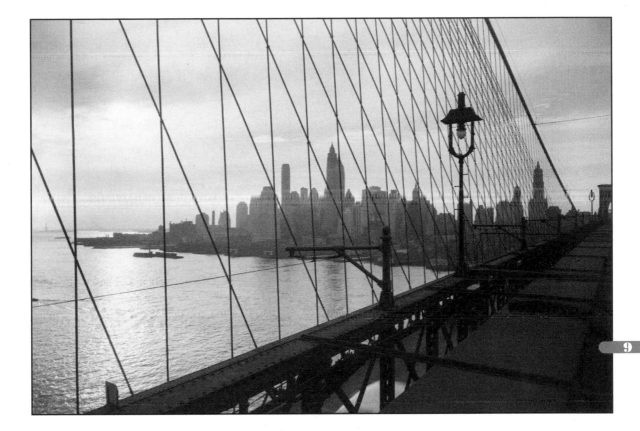

Angles of Literacy

Reading can be just like a conversation. A writer "talks" and you "listen," trying to figure out what the writer is saying to you. This is what literacy is all about—not just reading, but understanding and interacting with what you read. In this *Daybook*, you will learn how to hold up your end of the conversation.

Marking and highlighting the text, connecting what you read to your own experiences, trying to look through the eyes of the writer to discover his or her perspective, studying the writer's language and craft—these are all strategies you can use to turn your reading experiences into conversations with literature.

Imagine you are talking to a friend who hums and looks around the room as you try to engage her in a conversation. She probably doesn't hear a word you say. When you're reading, be careful not to do the same thing. Instead of tuning out and letting your mind go elsewhere, zero in on what you're reading and become involved.

- Circle words that are new to you and underline key phrases.
- Note word patterns and repetition (especially in poetry).
- In the margin, write down your questions and reactions to the work.

When you get involved, not only will you pay attention to your conversation with the writer, you'll gain a much better understanding of what you are reading. As you read "Alabama Earth," notice how one reader interacted with the text.

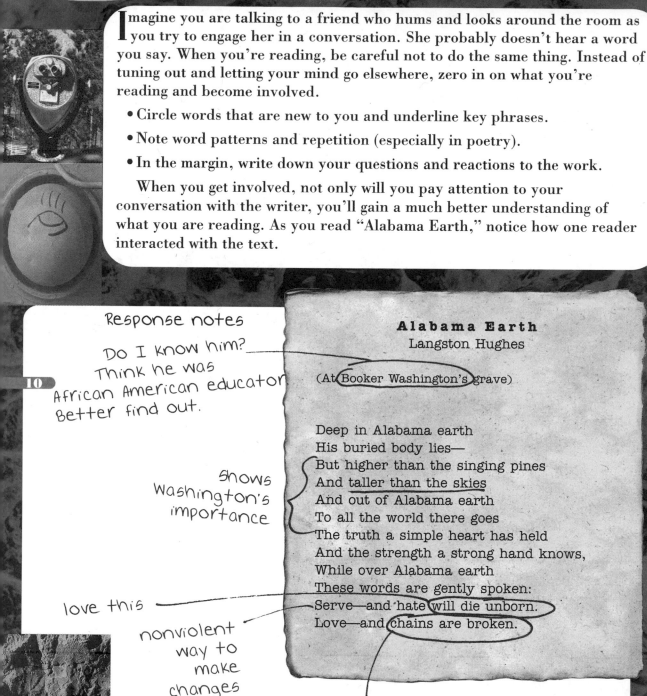

Response notes

Do I know him? Think he was African American educator. Better find out.

Shows Washington's importance

love this

nonviolent way to make changes

Alabama Earth
Langston Hughes

(At Booker Washington's grave)

Deep in Alabama earth
His buried body lies—
But higher than the singing pines
And taller than the skies
And out of Alabama earth
To all the world there goes
The truth a simple heart has held
And the strength a strong hand knows,
While over Alabama earth
These words are gently spoken:
Serve—and hate will die unborn.
Love—and chains are broken.

Huh?

As you read "Theme for English B," another poem by Langston Hughes, use strategies to become actively involved in the poem. Mark vocabulary and concepts that are new to you. Underline phrases that tell you more about the speaker and subject of the poem. In the margin, write any questions or reactions you have to the poem.

Theme for English B
Langston Hughes

The instructor said,

> Go home and write
> a page tonight.
> And let that page come out of you—
> Then, it will be true.

I wonder if it's that simple?
I am twenty-two, colored, born in Winston-Salem.
I went to school there, then Durham, then here
to this college on the hill above Harlem.
I am the only colored student in my class.
The steps from the hill lead down into Harlem,
through a park, then I cross St. Nicholas,
Eighth Avenue, Seventh, and I come to the Y,
the Harlem Branch Y, where I take the elevator
up to my room, sit down, and write this page:

It's not easy to know what is true for you or me
at twenty-two, my age. But I guess I'm what
I feel and see and hear, Harlem, I hear you:
hear you, hear me—we two—you, me, talk on this page.
(I hear New York, too.) Me—who?
Well, I like to eat, sleep, drink, and be in love.
I like to work, read, learn, and understand life.
I like a pipe for a Christmas present,
or records—Bessie, bop, or Bach.
I guess being colored doesn't make me *not* like
the same things other folks like who are other races.
So will my page be colored that I write?
Being me, it will not be white.
But it will be
a part of you, instructor.
You are white—
yet a part of me, as I am a part of you.
That's American.
Sometimes perhaps you don't want to be a part of me.
Nor do I often want to be a part of you.
But we are, that's true!
As I learn from you,
I guess you learn from me—
although you're older—and white—
and somewhat more free.

This is my page for English B.

●◆ What is the theme or meaning of Langston Hughes's "Theme for English B"? Use your response notes to help you reflect on the poem's meaning.

●◆ How do you think your "conversation" with the poem helped you understand it better? Discuss your thoughts with a partner. Then summarize your discussion below.

As an active reader, jot down notes, mark up the text, and ask questions. This helps you better understand and respond to a work of literature.

Two

Connecting to the Story

Have you ever read something that seems like it was written just for you? Most likely, there was something in the piece that you were able to connect to your own experiences or feelings. You might, for example, connect a piece of writing to something else you have read, to an event you have seen or heard about, or to something that has happened to you. When you take the time to make these connections, you gain a better understanding of the subject of the writing.

As you read "Aunt Sue's Stories," jot down in the margin anything that reminds you of someone you know or something that you have read, heard about, or experienced.

Aunt Sue's Stories
Langston Hughes

Aunt Sue has a head full of stories.
Aunt Sue has a whole heart full of stories.
Summer nights on the front porch
Aunt Sue cuddles a brown-faced child to her bosom
And tells him stories.

Black slaves
Working in the hot sun,
And black slaves
Walking in the dewy night,
And black slaves
Singing sorrow songs on the banks of a mighty river
Mingle themselves softly
In the flow of old Aunt Sue's voice,
Mingle themselves softly
In the dark shadows that cross and recross
Aunt Sue's stories.

And the dark-faced child, listening,
Knows that Aunt Sue's stories are real stories.
He knows that Aunt Sue never got her stories
Out of any book at all,
But that they came
Right out of her own life.
The dark-faced child is quiet
Of a summer night
Listening to Aunt Sue's stories.

Response notes

like my
grandfather

13

●◆Describe in three or four sentences any connections you can think of between you and "Aunt Sue's Stories."

....

....

....

....

....

....

●◆Imagine that you are a member of Aunt Sue's family. Make a photo album about your family's history. What would you write near her photo? Write a caption, telling what Aunt Sue means to you and why she is an important part of the family.

Comparing your own experiences to the events in a piece of literature helps you become more involved with the text.

Three
Language and Craft

Anyone who knows how to write can be a writer. But what makes some writing more intriguing? more interesting? more suspenseful? more descriptive? Good writers know how to use language and craft to turn words on a page into something that captures readers and draws them in. Language and craft involves a variety of elements, including an author's:

- choice of words
- use of **figurative language**
- writing **style**
- use of sound

As you read "The Weary Blues," jot down your impressions of how Langston Hughes uses these and other elements of language and craft.

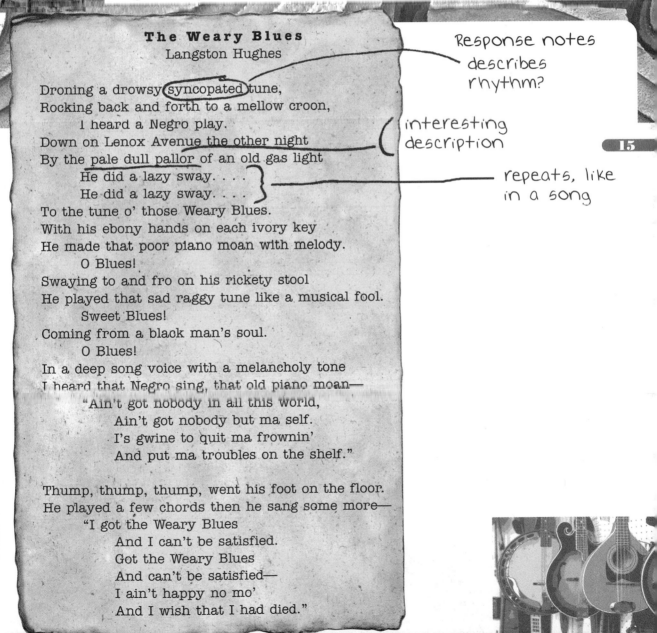

The Weary Blues
Langston Hughes

Droning a drowsy syncopated tune,
Rocking back and forth to a mellow croon,
    I heard a Negro play.
Down on Lenox Avenue the other night
By the pale dull pallor of an old gas light
    He did a lazy sway. . . .
    He did a lazy sway. . . .
To the tune o' those Weary Blues.
With his ebony hands on each ivory key
He made that poor piano moan with melody.
    O Blues!
Swaying to and fro on his rickety stool
He played that sad raggy tune like a musical fool.
    Sweet Blues!
Coming from a black man's soul.
    O Blues!
In a deep song voice with a melancholy tone
I heard that Negro sing, that old piano moan—
    "Ain't got nobody in all this world,
        Ain't got nobody but ma self.
        I's gwine to quit ma frownin'
        And put ma troubles on the shelf."

Thump, thump, thump, went his foot on the floor.
He played a few chords then he sang some more—
    "I got the Weary Blues
        And I can't be satisfied.
        Got the Weary Blues
        And can't be satisfied—
        I ain't happy no mo'
        And I wish that I had died."

Response notes describes rhythm?

interesting description

repeats, like in a song

15

THE WEARY BLUES (continued)

And far into the night he crooned that tune.
The stars went out and so did the moon.
The singer stopped playing and went to bed
While the Weary Blues echoed through his head.
He slept like a rock or a man that's dead.

●◆ Think about how Langston Hughes adapted his language to the subject and purpose of his work. In the chart below, record your ideas about language and craft in "The Weary Blues" and "Theme for English B."

	"The Weary Blues"	"Theme for English B"
What is the effect of Hughes's choice of words in the poem?		
16 Does Hughes use figurative language (such as similes and metaphors)? What does it add to the poem?		
What is the style of the poem (for example, is it conversational)? How does the style affect you as you read?		
How do sound devices reflect the meaning of the poem?		

Pay special attention to a writer's word choice and the way that words are arranged. This will help you understand what the writer is trying to convey about a subject.

Four
An Author's Perspective

Writers see the same subject in different ways because of their perspectives. A writer's perspective is shaped by his or her experiences, education, feelings, and so on. A poet who lives in Canada might have a different perspective on snow, for example, than a poet living in Arizona. These two poets' poems about snow would probably be entirely different—and shaped by their own experiences (or inexperience) with winter.

Langston Hughes introduced his fictional character, Jesse B. Simple, in a newspaper column he wrote for the *Chicago Defender,* a newspaper owned by African Americans that began in the 1940s. Through Simple, Hughes showed events from his perspective. As you read, **highlight** sections that reveal clues to Hughes's perspective.

---

from *The Return of Simple* by Langston Hughes

Response notes

"Next week is Negro History Week," said Simple. "And how much Negro history do you know?"

"Why should I know *Negro* history?" I replied. "I am an American."

"But you are also a black man," said Simple, "and you did not come over on the *Mayflower*—at least, not the same *Mayflower* as the rest."

"What rest?" I asked.

"The rest who make up the most," said Simple, "then write the history books and leave *us* out, or else put in the books nothing but prize fighters and ballplayers. Some folks think Negro history begins and ends with Jackie Robinson."

"Not quite," I said.

"Not quite is right," said Simple. "Before Jackie there was Du Bois and before him there was Booker T. Washington, and before him was Frederick Douglass and before Douglass the original Freedom Walker, Harriet Tubman, who were a lady. Before her was them great Freedom Fighters who started rebellions in the South long before the Civil War. By name they was Gabriel and Nat Turner and Denmark Vesey."

"When, how, and where did you get all that information at once?" I asked.

"From my wife, Joyce," said Simple. "Joyce is a fiend for history. She belongs to the Association for the Study of Negro Life and History. Also Joyce went to school down South. There colored teachers teach children about *our* history. It is not like up North where almost no teachers teach children anything about themselves and who they is and where they come from out of our great black past which were Africa in the old days."

"The days of Ashanti and Benin and the great trade

17

routes in the Middle Ages, the great cities and great kings."

"Amen!" said Simple. "It might have been long ago, but we had black kings. It is from one of them kings that I am descended."

"You?" I exclaimed. "How so? After five hundred years it hardly seems possible that you can trace your ancestry back to an African king."

"Oh, but I can," said Simple. "It is only just a matter of simple arithmetic. Suppose great old King Ashanti in his middle ages had one son. And that one son had two sons. And them two sons each had three sons—and so on down the line, each bigger set of sons having bigger sets of children themselves. Why, the way them sons of kings and kings' sons multiplied, after five hundred years, every black man in the U.S.A. must be the son of one of them African king's grandsons' sons—including me. A matter of simple arithmetic—I am descended from a king."

"It is a good thing to think, anyhow," I said.

"Furthermore, I am descended from the people who built the pyramids, created the alphabets, first wrote words on stones, and first added up two and two."

"Who said all those wise men were colored?"

"Joyce, my wife—and I never doubts her word. She has been going to the Schomburg Collection all week reading books which she cannot take out and carry home because they is too valuable to the Negro people, so must be read in the library. In some places in Harlem a rat might chaw one of them books which is so old and so valuable nobody could put it back in the library. My wife says the Schomburg in Harlem is one of the greatest places in the world to find out about Negro history. Joyce tried to drag me there one day, but I said I had rather get my history from her after she has got it from what she calls the archives. Friend, what is an archive?"

"A place of recorded records, books, files, the materials in which history is preserved."

"They got a million archives in the Schomburg library," said Simple.

"By no stretch of the imagination could there be that many."

"Yes there is," said Simple. "Every word in there is an archive to the Negro people, and to me. I want to know about my kings, my past, my Africa, my history years that make me proud. I want to go back to the days when I did not have to knock and bang and beg at doors for the chance to do things like I do now. I want to go back to the days of my blackness and

18

from ***The Return of Simple*** by Langston Hughes

Response notes

greatness when I were in my own land and were king and I invented arithmetic."

"The way you can multiply kings and produce yourself as a least common denominator, maybe you did invent arithmetic," I said.

"Maybe I did," said Simple.

What does this article reveal about Hughes's perspective?

Suppose you are compiling an anthology of the works of Langston Hughes, and it will include everything you have read in this unit. Write an introduction to the anthology. Explain what you know about Hughes, his perspective, what his works reveal about him, and his purposes for writing.

19

> Understanding an author's perspective helps you figure out what the author is trying to "tell" you in a piece of writing.

Five

Focus on the Writer

Knowing about an author's life can help you better understand the writer's works of literature. Not every story, poem, or article that a writer composes is autobiographical, but most writers include bits and pieces of their own experiences, memories, and so forth in their writing. When you know something about writers' experiences and concerns, you gain important insights not only into their lives, but also into their craft and writing.

As you read from Langston Hughes's autobiography, jot down in the margins any connections you find between his life and his works.

Response notes

from *I Wonder As I Wander* by Langston Hughes

I came out of college in 1929, the year of the Stock Market crash and the beginning of the Great Depression. I had written my first novel, *Not Without Laughter,* as a student on the campus of Lincoln University. I had had a scholarship to college. After graduation a monthly sum from my patron enabled me to live comfortably in suburban New Jersey, an hour from Manhattan, revising my novel at leisure. Propelled by the backwash of the "Harlem Renaissance" of the early 'twenties, I had been drifting along pleasantly on the delightful rewards of my poems which seemed to please the fancy of kind-hearted New York ladies with money to help young writers. The magazines used very few stories with Negro themes, since Negro themes were considered exotic, in a class with Chinese or East Indian features. Editorial offices then never hired Negro writers to read manuscripts or employed them to work on their staffs. Almost all the young white writers I'd known in New York in the 'twenties had gotten good jobs with publishers or magazines as a result of their creative work. White friends of mine in Manhattan, whose first novels had received reviews nowhere nearly so good as my own, had been called to Hollywood, or were doing scripts for the radio. Poets whose poetry sold hardly at all had been offered jobs on smart New York magazines. But they were white. I was colored. So in Haiti I began to puzzle out how I, *a Negro,* could make a living in America from writing.

There was one other dilemma—how to make a living from *the kind of writing I wanted to do.* I did not want to write for the pulps, or turn out fake "true" stories to sell under anonymous names as Wallace Thurman did. I did not want to bat out slick non-Negro short stories in competition with a thousand other commercial writers trying to make *The*

from *I Wonder As I Wander* by Langston Hughes

Saturday Evening Post. I wanted to write seriously and as well as I knew how about the Negro people, and make *that* kind of writing earn for me a living.

I thought, with the four hundred dollars my novel had given me, I had better go sit in the sun awhile and think, having just been through a tense and disheartening winter after a series of misunderstandings with the kind lady who had been my patron. She wanted me to be more African than Harlem—primitive in the simple, intuitive and noble sense of the word. I couldn't be, having grown up in Kansas City, Chicago and Cleveland. So that winter had left me ill in my soul.

■◆ Create a timeline of Hughes's life. List four or five key events of his life. Beneath the timeline, explain whether any of these events are reflected in Hughes's article or poems.

21

●◆Langston Hughes won numerous awards for his writing. Imagine you are introducing him at an awards ceremony. Write your introduction. Tell about Hughes's beginnings as a writer, the obstacles he overcame, and the messages that he conveys in his work. Why is he worthy of the award?

Keeping in mind what you know about an author will help you connect the writer and his or her work.

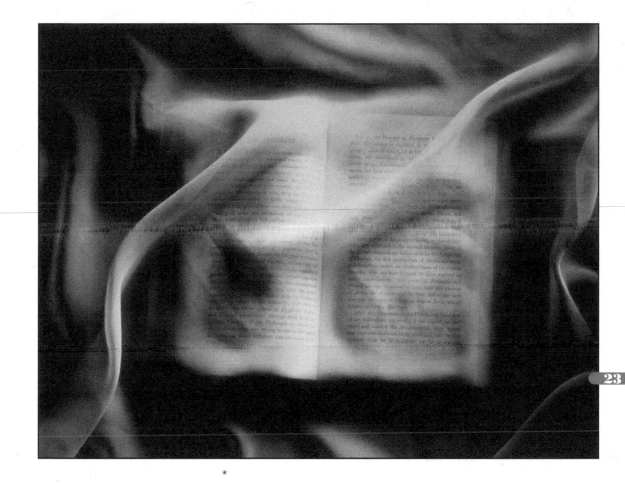

Essentials of Reading

Reading might seem like second nature to you—after all, you've been doing it for years. But what separates your reading now from when you began learning how to read? You are able to read <u>actively</u> and to interact with a story rather than just struggle to figure out the words.

In this unit, you'll strengthen your ability to use a variety of important reading strategies. These essentials include making predictions and inferences, determining the main idea, and evaluating and reflecting on what you've read. Using these strategies will help you better understand what you read. They can also help you become more connected with a text—to become a participant, rather than an outside observer.

Making Predictions

Can you imagine riding a bike without looking ahead to see what's coming up? Not only would it take a lot of the fun out of the ride, it would also be dangerous. When you don't "look ahead" while reading, you're obviously not putting yourself in danger. But you are neglecting a useful strategy: making **predictions**. As you read, stop and ask yourself at different points in the story, "What is going to happen next?" As you answer that question, make sure that your predictions "match" the text of the story and make sense.

In the excerpt below, the **narrator**, Marguerite, describes her graduation from eighth grade. As you read, jot down your predictions in the response notes.

RESPONSE NOTES

from *I Know Why the Caged Bird Sings* by Maya Angelou

Amazingly the great day finally dawned and I was out of bed before I knew it. I threw open the back door to see it more clearly, but Momma said, "Sister, come away from that door and put your robe on."

I hoped the memory of that morning would never leave me. Sunlight was itself still young, and the day had none of the insistence maturity would bring it in a few hours. In my robe and barefoot in the backyard, under cover of going to see about my new beans, I gave myself up to the gentle warmth and thanked God that no matter what evil I had done in my life He had allowed me to live to see this day. Somewhere in my fatalism I had expected to die, accidentally, and never have the chance to walk up the stairs in the auditorium and gracefully receive my hard-earned diploma. Out of God's merciful bosom I had won reprieve.

Bailey came out in his robe and gave me a box wrapped in Christmas paper. He said he had saved his money for months to pay for it. It felt like a box of chocolates, but I knew Bailey wouldn't save money to buy candy when we had all we could want under our noses.

He was as proud of the gift as I. It was a soft-leather-bound copy of a collection of poems by Edgar Allan Poe, or, as Bailey and I called him, "Eap." I turned to "Annabel Lee" and we walked up and down the garden rows, the cool dirt between our toes, reciting the beautifully sad lines.

Momma made a Sunday breakfast although it was only Friday. After we finished the blessing, I opened my eyes to find the watch on my plate. It was a dream of a day. Everything went smoothly and to my credit, I didn't have to be reminded or scolded for anything. Near evening I was too jittery to attend to chores, so Bailey volunteered to do all before his bath.

24

from *I Know Why the Caged Bird Sings* by Maya Angelou

Days before, we had made a sign for the Store, and as we turned out the lights Momma hung the cardboard over the door-knob. It read clearly: CLOSED. GRADUATION.

My dress fitted perfectly and everyone said that I looked like a sunbeam in it. On the hill, going toward the school, Bailey walked behind with Uncle Willie, who muttered, "Go on, Ju." He wanted him to walk ahead with us because it embarrassed him to have to walk so slowly. Bailey said he'd let the ladies walk together, and the men would bring up the rear. We all laughed, nicely.

Little children dashed by out of the dark like fireflies. Their crepe-paper dresses and butterfly wings were not made for running and we heard more than one rip, dryly, and the regretful "uh uh" that followed.

●❖Based on what that narrator has said so far, what do you think graduation will be like for her and her graduating class?

....

....

25

....

Go back into the story and circle clues that led you to this prediction. Then continue reading.

The school blazed without gaiety. The windows seemed cold and unfriendly from the lower hill. A sense of ill-fated timing crept over me, and if Momma hadn't reached for my hand I would have drifted back to Bailey and Uncle Willie, and possibly beyond. She made a few slow jokes about my feet getting cold, and tugged me along to the now-strange building.

Around the front steps, assurance came back. There were my fellow "greats," the graduating class. Hair brushed back, legs oiled, new dresses and pressed pleats, fresh pocket handkerchiefs and little handbags, all homesewn. Oh, we were up to snuff, all right. I joined my comrades and didn't even see my family go in to find seats in the crowded auditorium.

The school band struck up a march and all classes filed in as had been rehearsed. We stood in front of our seats, as assigned, and on a signal from the choir director, we sat. No sooner had this been accomplished than the band started to play the national anthem. We rose again and sang the song, after which we recited the pledge of allegiance. We remained standing for a brief minute before the choir director and the principal signaled to us, rather desperately I thought, to take our seats. The command was so unusual that our carefully rehearsed and smooth-running machine was thrown off. For a full minute we fumbled for our chairs and bumped into each other awkwardly. Habits change or solidify under pressure, so in our state of nervous tension we had been ready to follow our usual assembly pattern: the American national anthem, then the pledge of allegiance, then the song every Black person I knew called the Negro National Anthem. All done in the same key, with the same passion and most often standing on the same foot.

Finding my seat at last, I was overcome with a presentiment of worse things to come. Something unrehearsed, unplanned, was going to happen, and we were going to be made to look bad. I distinctly remember being explicit in the choice of pronoun. It was "we," the graduating class, the unit, that concerned me then.

The principal welcomed "parents and friends" and asked the Baptist minister to lead us in prayer. His invocation was brief and punchy, and for a second I thought we were getting back on the high road to right action. When the principal came back to the dais, however, his voice had changed. Sounds always affected me profoundly and the principal's voice was one of my favorites. During assembly it melted and lowed weakly into the audience. It had not been in my plan to listen to him, but my curiosity was piqued and I straightened up to give him my attention.

He was talking about Booker T. Washington, our "late great leader," who said we can be as close as the fingers on the hand, etc. . . . Then he said a few vague things about friendship and the friendship of kindly people to those less fortunate than themselves. With that his voice nearly faded, thin, away. Like a river diminishing to a stream and then to a trickle. But he cleared his throat and said, "Our speaker tonight, who is also our friend, came from Texarkana to deliver the commencement address, but due to the irregularity of the train schedule, he's going to, as they say, 'speak and run.'" He said that we understood and wanted the man to know that we were most grateful for the time he was able to give us and then something about how we were willing always to adjust to another's program and without more ado—"I give you Mr. Edward Donleavy."

●◆ **What do you think will happen next?**

from *I Know Why the Caged Bird Sings* by Maya Angelou

→ Response notes →

Not one but two white men came through the door offstage. The shorter one walked to the speaker's platform, and the tall one moved over to the center seat and sat down. But that was our principal's seat, and already occupied. The dislodged gentleman bounced around for a long breath or two before the Baptist minister gave him his chair, then with more dignity than the situation deserved, the minister walked off the stage.

Donleavy looked at the audience once (on reflection, I'm sure that he wanted only to reassure himself that we were really there), adjusted his glasses and began to read from a sheaf of papers.

He was glad "to be here and to see the work going on just as it was in the other schools."

At the first "Amen" from the audience I willed the offender to immediate death by choking on the word. But Amens and Yes, sir's began to fall around the room like rain through a ragged umbrella.

He told us of the wonderful changes we children in Stamps had in store. The Central School (naturally, the white school was Central) had already been granted improvements that would be in use in the fall. A well-known artist was coming from Little Rock to teach art to them. They were going to have the newest microscopes and chemistry equipment for their laboratory. Mr. Donleavy didn't leave us long in the dark over who made these improvement available to Central High. Nor were we to be ignored in the general betterment scheme he had in mind.

He said that he had pointed out to people at a very high level that one of the first-line football tacklers at Arkansas Agricultural and Mechanical College had graduated from good old Lafayette County Training School. Here fewer Amen's were heard. Those few that did break through lay dully in the air with the heaviness of habit.

He went on to praise us. He went on to say how he had bragged that "one of the best basketball players at Fisk sank his first ball right here at Lafayette County Training School."

The white kids were going to have a chance to become Galileos and Madame Curies and Edisons and Gauguins, and our boys (the girls weren't even in on it) would try to be Jesse Owenses and Joe Louises.

Owens and the Brown Bomber were great heroes in our world, but what school official in the white-goddom of Little Rock had the right to decide that those two men must be our only heroes? Who decided that for Henry Reed to become a scientist he had to work like George Washington Carver, as a bootblack, to buy a lousy microscope? Bailey was obviously

27

from *I Know Why the Caged Bird Sings* by Maya Angelou

always going to be too small to be an athlete, so which concrete angel glued to what country seat had decided that if my brother wanted to become a lawyer he had to first pay penance for his skin by picking cotton and hoeing corn and studying correspondence books at night for twenty years?

❧ What do you think will happen next at the graduation ceremony? Write your prediction, as if it already happened, in an account for the school newspaper. Be sure that your prediction is consistent with what has already happened in the story.

Daily News

As you read, look for clues that point to what will happen next. Base your predictions on details in the text to be sure that your predictions make sense.

Two
Between the Lines

When you read, you and the writer are partners. The writer provides you with details, or "clues," and you use these clues to determine what's going on in the selection. Writers aren't trying to trick you. Instead, they are providing clues to help you make **inferences** or reasonable guesses. This partnership between writer and reader helps you become actively involved in what you read. As you read more of *I Know Why the Caged Bird Sings*, jot down what you can infer about the narrator's feelings about her education. Circle details in the story that lead you to those inferences.

from ***I Know Why the Caged Bird Sings*** by Maya Angelou

Response notes

My name had lost its ring of familiarity and I had to be nudged to go and receive my diploma. All my preparations had fled. I neither marched up to the stage like a conquering Amazon, nor did I look in the audience for Bailey's nod of approval. Marguerite Johnson, I heard the name again, my honors were read, there were noises in the audience of appreciation, and I took my place on the stage as rehearsed.

I thought about colors I hated: ecru, puce, lavender, beige and black.

There was shuffling and rustling around me, then Henry Reed was giving his valedictory address, "To Be or Not to Be." Hadn't he heard the whitefolks? We couldn't *be*, so the question was a waste of time. Henry's voice came out clear and strong. I feared to look at him. Hadn't he got the message? There was no "nobler in the mind" for Negroes because the world didn't think we had minds, and they let us know it. "Outrageous fortune"? Now, that was a joke. When the ceremony was over I had to tell Henry Reed some things. That is, if I still cared. Not "rub," Henry, "erase." "Ah, there's the erase." Us.

Henry had been a good student in elocution. His voice rose on tides of promise and fell on waves of warnings. The English teacher had helped him to create a sermon winging through Hamlet's soliloquy. To be a man, a doer, a builder, a leader, or to be a tool, an unfunny joke, a crusher of funky toadstools. I marveled that Henry could go through with the speech as if we had a choice.

I had been listening and silently rebutting each sentence with my eyes closed; then there was a hush, which in an audience warns that something unplanned is happening. I looked up and saw Henry Reed, the conservative, the proper, the A student, turn his back to the audience and turn to us (the proud graduating class of 1940) and sing, nearly speaking,

29

Response notes

"Lift ev'ry voice and sing
Till earth and heaven ring
Ring with the harmonies of Liberty . . ."
It was the poem written by James Weldon Johnson. It was
the music composed by J. Rosamond Johnson. It was the Negro
national anthem. Out of habit we were singing it.

Our mothers and fathers stood in the dark hall and joined
the hymn of encouragement. A kindergarten teacher led the
small children onto the stage and the buttercups and daisies
and bunny rabbits marked time and tried to follow:
"Stony the road we trod
Bitter the chastening rod
Felt in the days when hope, unborn, had died.
Yet with a steady beat
Have not our weary feet
Come to the place for which our fathers sighed?"
Every child I knew had learned that song with his ABC's
and along with "Jesus Loves Me This I Know." But I personally
had never heard it before. Never heard the words, despite the
thousand of times I had sung them. Never thought they had
anything to do with me.

On the other hand, the words of Patrick Henry had made
such an impression on me that I had been able to stretch
myself tall and trembling and say, "I know not what course
others may take, but as for me, give me liberty or give me
death."

And now I heard, really for the first time:
"We have come over a way that with tears
has been watered,
We have come, treading our path through
the blood of the slaughtered."
While echoes of the song shivered in the air, Henry Reed
bowed his head, said "Thank you," and returned to his place in
the line. The tears that slipped down many faces were not
wiped away in shame.

●◆Think back to the news article you wrote about the rest of the graduation
ceremony. Compare your ending to what actually happens.

●◆ Create a web. In the center of the web, write down a word or two to describe the meaning of graduation to the narrator. On arms extending from the web, write clues from the story that lead you to this inference.

graduation =

●◆ Based on the excerpts and your web, make an inference (or inferences) about what graduation means to Angelou. Write a paragraph that explains your inference and supports it with "proof" from the selection.

31

Look for details in the text that help you make inferences about characters and events.

The Main Idea

Writers rely on their readers to get the point they are trying to make. Rather than saying, "This is what I want you to know," a writer selects and organizes material to convey a **main idea**—the "big idea" that the writer wants you to remember after you read.

In the following excerpt from *Now Is Your Time!*, Walter Dean Myers describes a court case, *Brown vs. Board of Education of Topeka*. This case challenged the ruling that "separate but equal" schools for black and white students were constitutional. Thurgood Marshall was the attorney who spearheaded the case against segregation. As you read, reflect on what points Myers wants to make about this topic.

from *Now Is Your Time!* by Walter Dean Myers

Response notes

It was Thurgood Marshall and a battery of N.A.A.C.P. attorneys who began to challenge segregation throughout the country. These men and women were warriors in the cause of freedom for African Americans, taking their battles into courtrooms across the country. They understood the process of American justice and the power of the Constitution.

In *Brown vs. Board of Education of Topeka*, Marshall argued that segregation was a violation of the Fourteenth Amendment—that even if the facilities and all other "tangibles" were equal, which was the heart of the case in *Plessy vs. Ferguson*, a violation still existed. There were intangible factors, he argued, that made the education unequal.

Everyone involved understood the significance of the case: that it was much more than whether black children could go to school with white children. If segregation in the schools was declared unconstitutional, then *all* segregation in public places could be declared unconstitutional.

Southerners who argued against ending school segregation were caught up, as then-Congressman Brooks Hays of Arkansas put it, in "a lifetime of adventures in that gap between law and custom." The law was one thing, but most Southern whites felt just as strongly about their customs as they did the law.

Dr. Kenneth B. Clark, an African-American psychologist, testified for the N.A.A.C.P. He presented clear evidence that the effect of segregation was harmful to African-American children. Describing studies conducted by black and white psychologists over a twenty-year period, he showed that black children felt inferior to white children. In a particularly dramatic study that he had supervised, four dolls, two white and two black, were presented to African-American children. From the responses of the children to the dolls, identical in

from *Now Is Your Time* by Walter Dean Myers

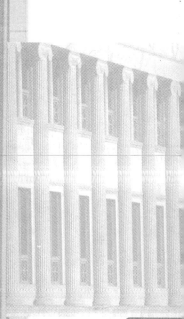

every way except color, it was clear that the children were rejecting the black dolls. African-American children did not just feel separated from white children, they felt that the separation was based on their inferiority.

Dr. Clark understood fully the principles and ideas of those people who had held Africans in bondage and had tried to make slaves of captives. By isolating people of African descent, by barring them from certain actions or places, they could make them feel inferior. The social scientists who testified at *Brown vs. Board of Education* showed that children who felt inferior also performed poorly.

The Justice Department argued that racial segregation was objectionable to the Eisenhower Administration and hurt our relationships with other nations.

On May 17, 1954, after deliberating for nearly a year and a half, the Supreme Court made its ruling. The Court stated that it could not use the intentions of 1868, when the Fourteenth Amendment was passed, as a guide to its ruling, or even those of 1896, when the decision in *Plessy vs. Ferguson* was handed down. Chief Justice Earl Warren wrote:

> We must consider public education in the light of its full development and its present place in American life throughout the nation. We must look instead to the effect of segregation itself on public education.

The Court went on to say that "modern authority" supported the idea that segregation deprived African Americans of equal opportunity. "Modern authority" referred to Dr. Kenneth B. Clark and the weight of evidence that he and the other social scientists had presented.

The high court's decision in *Brown vs. Board of Education* signaled an important change in the struggle for civil rights. It signaled clearly that the legal prohibitions that oppressed African Americans would have to fall. Equally important was the idea that the nature of the fight for equality would change. Ibrahima, Cinqué, Nat Turner, and George Latimer had struggled for freedom by fighting against their captors or fleeing from them. The 54th had fought for African freedom on the battlefields of the Civil War. Ida B. Wells had fought for equality with her pen. Lewis H. Latimer and Meta Vaux Warrick had tried to earn equality with their work. In *Brown vs. Board of Education* Thurgood Marshall, Kenneth B. Clark, and the lawyers and social scientists, both black and white, who helped them had won for African Americans a victory that would bring them closer to full equality than they had ever been in North America. There would still be legal battles to be won, but the major struggle would be in the hearts and minds of people and "in that gap between law and custom."

33

●◆ What main idea do you think Walter Dean Myers wants you to understand? What details in the writing pointed you toward the main idea? Underline several of these details. Then sum up his main idea in a new title for the selection:

....

....

●◆ In the space below, create a graphic organizer, such as a chart or diagram, to show the relationship between Myers's main idea and his supporting details.

The main idea is the point that a writer wants to make. As you read, look for details that will help you determine what the writer wants you to think about the topic.

Four
Evaluating What You Read

Do you read books and see movies that friends recommend? People usually want to see the best movies or read the most interesting books, but how do you decide what's best? You do so by evaluating the work.

When you read, first decide whether or not you like the selection. Then determine why you feel this way. This not only helps you develop an **opinion**, it helps you understand the basis for your opinion—and helps you better understand what you read.

➠ On a scale of 1 to 10, with 1 being "totally disagree" and 10 being "totally agree," rate these two statements about the excerpt from *Now Is Your Time!* on pages 32–33. Give specific reasons for your ratings.

Statement	Rating	Reasons
I like this piece of writing.		
The subject matter is interesting.		

35

➠ What other important criteria can you think of for deciding if a piece of writing is one that's worth reading? Continue the chart by adding your own criteria statements. Use these statements to further evaluate *Now Is Your Time!*

Statement	Rating	Reasons

→ Suppose a classmate is looking for your advice. He or she wants to learn more about school segregation and how it affected people. Which piece would you recommend that your classmate read—*Now Is Your Time!* or *I Know Why the Caged Bird Sings*? Write your recommendation, being sure to give reasons to support it.

Evaluating a piece of writing helps you form an opinion and gives you a better understanding of the piece.

Five

Reflecting on a Writer's Words

What's the first thing you do when you read a new piece of writing? Some readers try to figure out what it means. Other readers try to connect the piece to their own lives, determining how it affects them. Both of these processes are part of reflecting. When you read a story, poem, or even a nonfiction article, reflecting on it helps you connect it to your own life and determine what meaning, if any, it has for you. As you read "Like Bookends," jot down your thoughts about the poem in the response notes.

Like Bookends
by Eve Merriam

Like bookends
my father at one side
my mother at the other

propping me up
but unable to read
what I feel.

Were they born with clothes on?
Born with rules on?

When we sit at the dinner table
we smooth our napkins into polite folds.
How was your day dear
   Fine
And how was yours dear
   Fine
And how was school
   The same

Only once in a while
when we're not trying so hard
when we're not trying at all
our napkins suddenly whirl away
and we float up to the ceiling
where we sing and dance until it hurts from laughing

and then we float down
with our napkin parachutes
and once again spoon our soup
and pass the bread please.

Response notes

37

●◆How do you feel about this poem?

....

....

....

....

●◆In a short journal entry, reflect on how this poem connects to your own experiences. Have you ever felt like the speaker? In what instances? Do you think that most families are like the one in this poem? Why or why not?

....

....

....

....

....

....

....

....

....

....

....

....

Reflecting
on a piece of writing and
connecting it to your own experiences
helps you figure out what it
means to you.

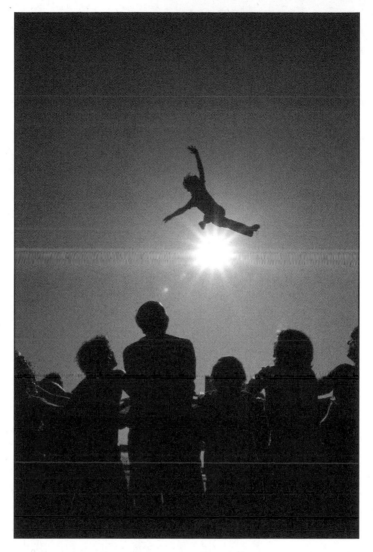

Essentials of Story

Writing a story is like constructing a building. While a building is assembled with beams, walls, and a roof, a story is produced with characters, a setting, and a theme. Just as buildings come in many different styles, from elaborate mansions to sleek skyscrapers to rustic farm-houses, stories can come in as many forms as there are writers to construct them.

But good writers know that there are "must-haves" for every story—the essentials of story: setting, character, point of view, plot, and theme. In this unit, you will learn how to recognize a well-constructed story—and how you can build your own.

One Where the Story Happens

Can you imagine a skyscraper built on a swamp? a day care center two steps from a highway? Just as a builder chooses the best place to construct a building, a writer must choose the best place to construct a story. The **setting** of a story is the time and place in which the story occurs. A writer might describe the setting directly—"It was a dark and stormy night"—or suggest the setting through the actions and the dialogue of the characters. Either way, the setting often helps establish the **mood** or feeling of a story.

When you read a story, form a picture in your mind of the setting. Think to yourself, "How does the writer bring the place to life? How does the setting reflect the overall mood or feeling of the story?" Jot down your thoughts in the response notes as you read this selection by Yoshiko Uchida.

Response notes

from *Journey to Topaz* by Yoshiko Uchida

The eager hopeful voices on the bus died down and soon stopped altogether. Mother said nothing more and Yuki herself grew silent. At the western rim of the desert they could see a tall range of mountains, but long before they reached their sheltering shadows the buses made a sharp left turn, and there in the midst of the desert, they came upon rows and rows of squat tar-papered barracks sitting in a pool of white dust that had once been the bottom of a lake. They had arrived at Topaz, the Central Utah War Relocation Center, which would be their new home.

Ken turned to look at Yuki. "Well, here we are," he said dryly. "This is beautiful Topaz."

The minute Yuki stepped off the bus, she felt the white powdery dust of the desert engulf her like a smothering blanket. The Boy Scout Drum and Bugle Corp had come out to welcome the incoming buses, but now they looked like flour-dusted cookies that had escaped from a bakery.

Yuki coughed while one of the team of doctors inspected her throat and then she ran quickly to talk to Emi while Ken finished registering the family.

"We've been assigned to Block 7, Barrack 2, Apartment C," she informed her. "Try to get the room next door."

Emi nodded. "OK, I'll tell Grandma," she said, for they both knew that if anybody could manage such an arrangement, Grandma could.

A boy about Ken's age offered to take them out to their new quarters. He had come in one of the earlier contingents and already knew his way around the big, sprawling barrack city.

"It's a mile square," he explained as they started toward

from *Journey to Topaz* by Yoshiko Uchida

Response notes

Block 7, and like a guide on a tour he told them all he knew about Topaz.

"There're forty-two blocks and each block has twelve barracks with a mess hall and a latrine-washroom in the center," he pointed out. "When the barracks are all finished and occupied, we'll be the fifth largest city in Utah."

"Imagine!" Mother said.

It sounded impressive, but Yuki thought she had never seen a more dreary place in all her life. There wasn't a single tree or a blade of grass to break the monotony of the sun-bleached desert. It was like the carcass of a chicken stripped clean of any meat and left all dry, brittle bone. The newly constructed road was still soft with churned up dust and they sank into it with each step as though they were plowing through a snow bank.

"Whoever built this camp wasn't very bright," Ken observed as they struggled along.

"Why?" Yuki asked, although she could think of several reasons herself. For one thing, she certainly wouldn't have covered all the barracks with black tarpaper. It made the camp look so bleak and uninviting. She would have painted the barracks all different colors. Maybe one block would be pink and lavender with rose-colored chimneys and roofs, and another block would be blue and green with some sunny yellow roofs. "Why?" she asked Ken again.

"If they'd left some of the greasewood growing, the roots would have held down some of the dust," he explained. "As it is, they've churned up this whole camp site like one big sack of loose flour."

"You're right," their guide agreed. "You should see one of our dust storms. You'll wish you'd never heard of Topaz when you've been in one of those."

Yuki shuddered. It sounded horrible. It was bad enough even without the wind, for the dust just hung in the air, sifting into her eyes and into her nose and mouth with each breath.

Mother was holding a handkerchief over her nose and mouth so Yuki could see only her eyes, her lashes fringed with dust. The sun blazed down on them making Yuki feel dry and parched deep down inside. Her heart felt shriveled and her lungs seemed to be drying up. Her head felt light, as though it were floating on somebody else's body, and when the guide said something about the altitude, his voice sounded far away.

"Well, here we are," he said at last.

41

●◆ In this description of setting, Uchida uses vivid **imagery** that appeals to both the reader's sense of sight and touch. In the chart below, note or sketch some of the images of sight and touch that Uchida uses to help readers clearly picture Topaz.

Images of sight	Images of touch

42

●◆ Describe the mood created by the setting of this piece. How does Uchida's choice of images add to this mood?

Two
What a Character

Often, stories that interest us have interesting or memorable **characters**. But how do we, as readers, learn about these characters? Rarely does the writer come right out and tell us all we need to know. Instead, writers let the character's words, thoughts, and actions, as well as the reactions of other characters, clue us in as to what the character is like.

In *The Witch of Blackbird Pond,* Kit Tyler is a newcomer to Connecticut Colony in 1687. As you read this excerpt, record your ideas about what kind of person Kit is in the response notes.

from ***The Witch of Blackbird Pond*** by Elizabeth George Speare

Response notes

She turned to watch the sailors stowing provisions into the longboat. She already regretted this impulsive trip ashore. There was no welcome for her at this chill Saybrook landing. She was grateful when at last the captain assembled the return group and she could climb back into the longboat. Four new passengers were embarking for the trip up the river, a shabby, dour-looking man and wife and their scrawny little girl clutching a wooden toy, and a tall, angular young man with a pale narrow face and shoulder-length fair hair under a wide-brimmed black hat. Captain Eaton took his place aft without attempting any introduction. The men readied their oars. Then Nathaniel, coming back down the road on a run, slipped the rope from the mooring and as they pulled away from the wharf leaped nimbly to his place with the crew.

They were halfway across the harbor when a wail of anguish broke from the child. Before anyone could stop her the little girl had flung herself to her knees and teetered dangerously over the edge of the boat. Her mother leaned forward, grasped the woolen jumper and jerked her back, smacking her down with a sharp cuff.

"Ma! The dolly's gone!" the child wailed. "The dolly Grandpa made for me!"

Kit could see the little wooden doll, its arms sticking stiffly into the air, bobbing helplessly in the water a few feet away.

"Shame on you!" the woman scolded. "After the work he went to. All that fuss for a toy, and then the minute you get one you throw it away!"

"I was holding her up to see the ship! Please get her back, Ma! Please! I'll never drop it again!"

The toy was drifting farther and farther from the boat, like a useless twig in the current. No one in the boat made a move, or paid the slightest attention. Kit could not keep silent.

from **The Witch of Blackbird Pond** by Elizabeth George Speare

"Turn back, Captain," she ordered impulsively. "'Twill be an easy thing to catch."

The captain did not even glance in her direction. Kit was not used to being ignored, and her temper flared. When a thin whimper from the child was silenced by a vicious cuff, her anger boiled over. Without a second's deliberation she acted. Kicking off her buckled shoes and dropping the woolen cloak, she plunged headlong over the side of the boat.

The shock of cold, totally unexpected, almost knocked her senseless. As her head came to the surface she could not catch her breath at all. But after a dazed second she sighted the bobbing piece of wood and instinctively struck out after it in vigorous strokes that set her blood moving again. She had the doll in her hand before her numbed mind realized that there had been a second splash, and as she turned back she saw that Nathaniel was in the water beside her, thrashing with a clumsy paddling motion. She could not help laughing as she passed him, and with a feeling of triumph she beat him to the boat. The captain leaned to drag her back over the side, and Nathaniel scrambled in behind her without any assistance.

"Such water!" she gasped. "I never dreamed water could be so cold!"

She shook back her wet hair, her cheeks glowing. But her laughter died away at sight of all their faces. Shock and horror and unmistakable anger stared back at her. Even Nathaniel's young face was dark with rage.

"You must be daft," the woman hissed. "To jump into the river and ruin those clothes!"

Kit tossed her head. "Bother the clothes! They'll dry. Besides, I have plenty of others."

"Then you might have a thought for somebody else!" snapped Nat, slapping the water out of his dripping breeches. "These are the only clothes I have."

Kit's eyes flashed. "Why did you jump in anyway? You needn't have bothered."

"You can be sure I wouldn't have," he retorted, "had I any idea you could swim."

Her eyes widened. "Swim?" she echoed scornfully. "Why my grandfather taught me to swim as soon as I could walk."

The others stared at her in suspicion. As though she had sprouted a tail and fins right before their eyes. What was the matter with these people? Not another word was uttered as the men pulled harder on their oars. A solid cloud of disapproval settled over the dripping girl, more chilling than the April breeze. Her high spirits plunged. She had made herself

44

from ***The Witch of Blackbird Pond*** by Elizabeth George Speare

Response notes

ridiculous. How many times had her grandfather cautioned her to think before she flew off the handle? She drew her knees and elbows tight under the red cloak and clenched her teeth to keep them from chattering. Water dripped off her matted hair and ran in icy trickles down her neck. Then, glancing defiantly from one hostile face to another, Kit found a small measure of comfort. The young man in the black hat was looking at her gravely, and all at once his lips twisted in spite of himself. A smile filled his eyes with such warmth and sympathy that a lump rose in Kit's throat, and she glanced away. Then she saw that the child, silently clutching her sodden doll, was staring at her with a gaze of pure worship.

●◆ **What is Kit Tyler like? Record a few of her personality traits in the chart. Include specific examples from the story to support your interpretation.**

What Kit Is Like	How I Know

45

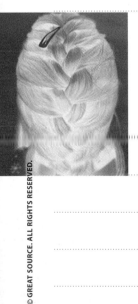

●◆ **Kit Tyler's story takes place more than 300 years ago. Discuss how Kit is similar to and different from people you know today.**

●◆Use the information you recorded in the chart on page 45 to write a character sketch of Kit. Imagine you are describing her for someone who has never read the story.

Look for clues to a character's personality from the actions, thoughts, and dialogue of the character, and the reactions of other characters.

Three
Who's Telling the Story?

When you read a story, you need to consider the **point of view**, or vantage point from which the story is told. Why is it important to consider this information? If the **narrator** is a character, the first-person point of view limits what you know to only what the narrator tells you. You may not know exactly how other characters are feeling. If a story is told by a third-person narrator, the point of view could still be *limited*: the narrator may choose to tell you only the thoughts of one or two characters. Sometimes the narrator is *omniscient*, or all-knowing—the narrator shares the thoughts of all the characters. Determining point of view helps you determine how much and what kind of information you are getting.

The Witch of Blackbird Pond is told from the third-person point of view. Return to the story. Is the narrator omniscient (all-knowing) or limited (telling the thoughts of only one or two characters)? How can you tell? Underline "proof" in the story.

●◆ What questions would you like to ask the narrator to get a better understanding of the events described? List them here.

47

●◆ Write about the incident in the excerpt from a different point of view. (For example, you might write a letter about the incident that Nathaniel would send to a friend, or describe it from the child's point of view.) Try to address some of your questions in your retelling of the incident.

Determine the point of view of a story. It will help you figure out whether the information you are getting about characters and events is from a limited or omniscient perspective.

Four The Plot

Without a **plot**—a sequence of events—there can be no story. Many stories follow the "classic" plot mountain, with the climax, or turning point, at the peak.

Climax

Rising Action

Falling Action

Exposition

Resoluton

But not every plot is a clear sequence of what happens first, second, and next. The plot may have turns, such as flashbacks or surprise events. As you read "Those Three Wishes," mark in the response notes any shifts in the plot to earlier scenes and plot events that surprise you. Think about the structure of this plot. If it's not a "mountain," then how would you describe it?

49

"Those Three Wishes" by Judith Gorog

Response notes

No one ever said that Melinda Alice was nice. That wasn't the word used. No, she was clever, even witty. She was called— never to her face, however—Melinda Malice. Melinda Alice was clever and cruel. Her mother, when she thought about it at all, hoped Melinda would grow out of it. To her father, Melinda's very good grades mattered.

It was Melinda Alice, back in the eighth grade, who had labeled the shy, myopic new girl "Contamination" and was the first to pretend that anything or anyone touched by the new girl had to be cleaned, inoculated, or avoided. High school had merely given Melinda Alice greater scope for her talents.

The surprising thing about Melinda Alice was her power; no one trusted her, but no one avoided her either. She was always included, always in the middle. If you had seen her, pretty and witty, in the center of a group of students walking past your house, you'd have thought, "There goes a natural leader."

Melinda Alice had left for school early. She wanted to study alone in a quiet spot she had because there was going to be a big math test, and Melinda Alice was not prepared. That A mattered; so Melinda Alice walked to school alone, planning her studies. She didn't usually notice nature much, so she nearly stepped on a beautiful snail that was making its way across the sidewalk.

"Ugh. Yucky thing," thought Melinda Alice, then stopped. Not wanting to step on the snail accidentally was one thing, but now she lifted her shoe to crush it.

"Please don't," said the snail.

"Why not?" retorted Melinda Alice.

"I'll give you three wishes," replied the snail evenly.

"Agreed," said Melinda Alice. "My first wish is that my next," she paused a split second, "my next thousand wishes come true." She smiled triumphantly and opened her bag to take out a small notebook and pencil to keep track.

Melinda Alice was sure she heard the snail say, "What a clever girl," as it made it to the safety of an ivy bed beside the sidewalk.

During the rest of the walk to school, Melinda Alice was occupied with wonderful ideas. She would have beautiful clothes. "Wish number two, that I will always be perfectly dressed," and she was just that. True, her new outfit was not a lot different from the one she had worn leaving the house, but that only meant Melinda Alice liked her own taste.

After thinking for awhile, she wrote, "Wish number three. I wish for pierced ears and small gold earrings." Her father had not allowed Melinda to have pierced ears, but now she had them anyway. She felt her new earrings and shook her beautiful hair in delight. "I can have anything: stereo, tapes, TV videodisc, moped, car, anything! All my life!" She hugged her books to herself in delight.

By the time she reached school, Melinda was almost an altruist; she could wish for peace. Then she wondered, "Is the snail that powerful?" She felt her ears, looked at her perfect blouse, skirt, jacket, shoes. "I could make ugly people beautiful, cure cripples . . . " She stopped. The wave of altruism had washed past. "I could pay people back who deserve it!" Melinda Alice looked at the school, at all the kids. She had an enormous sense of power. "They all have to do what I want now." She walked down the crowded halls to her locker. Melinda Alice could be sweet; she could be witty. She could— The bell rang for homeroom. Melinda Alice stashed her books, slammed the locker shut, and just made it to her seat.

"Hey, Melinda Alice," whispered Fred. "You know that big math test next period?"

"Oh, no," grimaced Melinda Alice. Her thoughts raced; "That damned snail made me late, and I forgot to study."

"I'll blow it," she groaned aloud. "I wish I were dead."

STRANGE

How does Judith Gorog organize the plot of "Those Three Wishes"?
Think of a graphic way to represent the plot, such as a timeline. On your
graphic, mark what you think are the major events of the story.

●●Use the information from your graphic to write a summary of the story.

52

As you read a story, take time to examine the main events of the plot. This will help you see the relationships between events of the story.

Were you able to write your summary using just the information from your graphic? If not, return to the graphic and add any missing information.

Five
The Theme

Fables are stories that have clear-cut lessons, or morals, at the end: "Don't count your chickens before they're hatched." "A penny saved is a penny earned." A theme is similar to a moral. The **theme** of a story is its underlying meaning or lesson about life. In a fable, the theme is often stated directly. In other stories, the themes might be implied and left for readers to figure out. Although a writer may have a theme in mind while writing a story, one reader may interpret the story differently than another. Often our interpretations of theme are based on our personal experiences.

➊❖Describe one theme or lesson about life you found in "Those Three Wishes."

●◆ Write a journal entry about an incident from your own life that relates
to this theme.

54

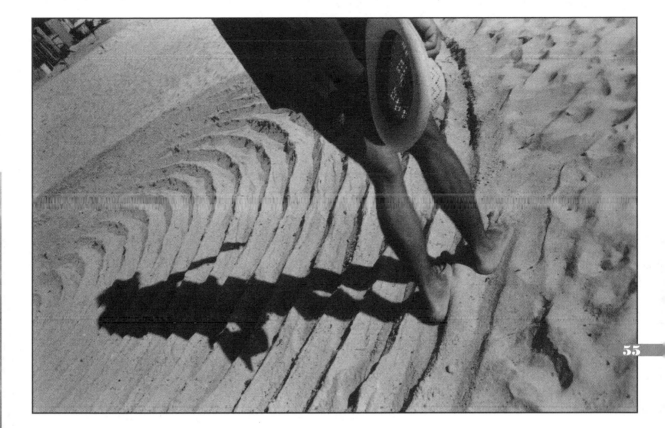

Understanding Theme

A well-written story can keep you on the edge of your seat, make you laugh, and make you cry—sometimes all at the same time. But stories and poems are usually meant to be more than just great escapes. Often, writing has something to "say" to us. The idea or point a writer is exploring through a poem or story is the **theme**, the underlying idea or meaning of a piece of writing.

As you look for themes in the literature you read, there may be more than one right "answer." In fact, a writer may try to convey more than one theme in a single selection. One way that you can think about theme is to imagine that you are having a conversation with the writer. Think to yourself, "What is the writer saying to me?" Chances are good that, when you "listen" and find the answer, you'll have found the theme.

The theme of a piece of writing is the author's underlying statement about life or human nature. Most of the time, the writer does not directly state the theme. Instead, you have to read between the lines and figure out what a piece of writing means. So how can you find the theme?

1. Read through the entire piece. As you read, ask, "What is the writer saying to me?"

2. Consider the details the writer emphasizes. If a certain character, for example, has something tragic happen as a result of personality flaws, what might the writer be trying to say?

3. Look at the way the writing is organized. Sometimes the writer says something about the theme at the end of a piece or in the first sentence of a paragraph.

Use these steps to figure out the theme or themes of the following excerpt.

Response notes

from ***Blacks*** by Gwendolyn Brooks

Maud Martha went east on Thirty-fourth Street, headed for Cottage Grove. It was August, and Thirty-fourth Street was all in bloom. The blooms, in their undershirts, sundresses and diapers, were hanging over porches and fence stiles and strollers, and were even bringing chairs out to the rims of the sidewalks.

At the corner of Thirty-fourth and Cottage Grove, a middle-aged blind man on a three-legged stool picked at a scarred guitar. The five or six patched and middle-aged men around him sang in husky, low tones, which carried the higher tone—ungarnished, insistent, at once a question and an answer—of the instrument.

Those men were going no further—and had gone nowhere. Tragedy.

She considered that word. On the whole, she felt, life was more comedy than tragedy. Nearly everything that happened had its comic element, not too well buried, either. Sooner or later one could find something to laugh at in almost every situation. That was what, in the last analysis, could keep folks from going mad. The truth was, if you got a good Tragedy out of a lifetime, one good, ripping tragedy, thorough, unridiculous, bottom-scraping, *not* the issue of human stupidity, you were doing, she thought, very well, you were doing well.

Look at the organization of the writing. Is there a place where you think Brooks states the theme—or gets pretty close to it? Put an "X" in the response notes near the spot.

➖◆ What do you think Brooks is trying to say to you about life? State the theme in a sentence or two.

➖◆ What details from the story point to the theme you identified? For each of these details from the story, jot down your ideas about how it supports the theme.

"blooms"   Young children are called blooms. Since blooms are cheerful and happy, this means that young children are doing well and haven't faced tragedy.

the middle-aged men

Maud Martha's thoughts about "Tragedy"

As you read a piece of writing, think to yourself, "What is the writer saying to me?" When you answer that question, you will know the theme.

Two Themes in Poems

Stories are not the only pieces of writing that have themes. In fact, poets often compose **poetry** just for the purpose of stating a message. And, unlike a story or novel in which the writer has a lot of space to develop the theme, a poet has to get to the point much more quickly. As you read a poem, you can use the same strategies for finding theme that you use when reading stories and other pieces of writing. In addition, look for **symbols** and images in poems that might contribute to the theme. As you read "Pete at the Zoo," write down any ideas about themes in the response notes.

Response notes

Pete at the Zoo
Gwendolyn Brooks

I wonder if the elephant
Is lonely in his stall
When all the boys and girls are gone
And there's no shout at all,
And there's no one to stamp before,
No one to note his might.
Does he hunch up, as I do,
Against the dark of night?

What images does the poem bring to mind? Sketch or describe what you see.

➤ What is the poet trying to say about life? How does the image of the elephant help suggest this idea?

59

➤ Reflect on the two questions below. Then record your ideas. Be sure your answers are consistent with the information in the poem.

What does this poem tell you about . . .

the speaker's feelings about herself?	the difference between how things "look" and what they actually are like?

As you read a poem, look for images that contribute to the theme. Deciding why the writer chose those particular images will help you discover the theme.

Three
Themes in Fables

In fables, the author often states a story's meaning in the moral at the end. The moral is sometimes—but not always—the same as the theme. Why would a writer do all of the "work" and tell you the point of the story? Writers directly state the moral of the fable so that readers have no doubts about the meaning or message of the selection.

As you will see as you read James Thurber's "The Princess and the Tin Box," the moral helps make the theme clear. Jot down your ideas about the theme as you read.

Response notes

"The Princess and the Tin Box" by James Thurber

Once upon a time, in a far country, there lived a king whose daughter was the prettiest princess in the world. Her eyes were like the cornflower, her hair was sweeter than the hyacinth, and her throat made the swan look dusty.

From the time she was a year old, the princess had been showered with presents. Her nursery looked like Cartier's window. Her toys were all made of gold or platinum or diamonds or emeralds. She was not permitted to have wooden blocks or china dolls or rubber dogs or linen books, because such materials were considered cheap for the daughter of a king.

When she was seven, she was allowed to attend the wedding of her brother and throw real pearls at the bride instead of rice. Only the nightingale, with his lyre of gold, was permitted to sing for the princess. The common blackbird, with his boxwood flute, was kept out of the palace grounds. She walked in silver-and-samite slippers to a sapphire-and-topaz bathroom and slept in an ivory bed inlaid with rubies.

On the day the princess was eighteen, the king sent a royal ambassador to the courts of five neighboring kingdoms to announce that he would give his daughter's hand in marriage to the prince who brought her the gift she liked the most.

The first prince to arrive at the palace rode a swift white stallion and laid at the feet of the princess an enormous apple made of solid gold which he had taken from a dragon who had guarded it for a thousand years. It was placed on a long ebony table set up to hold the gifts of the princess's suitors. The second prince, who came on a gray charger, brought her a nightingale made of a thousand diamonds, and it was placed beside the golden apple. The third prince, riding on a black horse, carried a great jewel box made of platinum and

"The Princess and the Tin Box" by James Thurber

Response notes

sapphires, and it was placed next to the diamond nightingale. The fourth prince, astride a fiery yellow horse, gave the princess a gigantic heart made of rubies and pierced by an emerald arrow. It was placed next to the platinum-and-sapphire jewel box.

Now the fifth prince was the strongest and handsomest of all the five suitors, but he was the son of a poor king whose realm had been overrun by mice and locusts and wizards and mining engineers so that there was nothing much of value left in it. He came plodding up to the palace of the princess on a plow horse and he brought her a small tin box filled with mica and feldspar and hornblende which he had picked up on the way.

The other princes roared with disdainful laughter when they saw the tawdry gift the fifth prince had brought to the princess. But she examined it with great interest and squealed with delight, for all her life she had been glutted with precious stones and priceless metals, but she had never seen tin before or mica or feldspar or hornblende. The tin box was placed next to the ruby heart pierced with an emerald arrow.

"Now," the king said to his daughter, "you must select the gift you like best and marry the prince that brought it."

The princess smiled and walked up to the table and picked up the present she liked the most. It was the platinum-and-sapphire jewel box, the gift of the third prince.

"The way I figure it," she said, "is this. It is a very large and expensive box, and when I am married, I will meet many admirers who will give me precious gems with which to fill it to the top. Therefore, it is the most valuable of all the gifts my suitors have brought me and I like it the best."

The princess married the third prince that very day in the midst of great merriment and high revelry. More than a hundred thousand pearls were thrown at her and she loved it.

Moral: All those who thought the princess was going to select the tin box filled with worthless stones instead of one of the other gifts will kindly stay after class and write one hundred times on the blackboard "I would rather have a hunk of aluminum silicate than a diamond necklace."

●◆ Did the moral of the story surprise you? Why or why not?

●◆ The ending of "The Princess and the Tin Box" surprises many readers. Yet the fable still has a clear theme, or meaning about life. What do you think it is?

●◆ What lesson could "The Princess and the Tin Box" teach if the ending were more "traditional"? Rewrite the end of the fable, having the princess choose a different suitor. At the end, state the theme that the new ending conveys.

62

The theme of a piece of writing is the author's underlying message about life. In fables, the moral can help you understand the theme.

Four
The Main Message

Imagine that you and three friends go to a movie. Afterwards, you are talking about what the movie means—and all four of you have different ideas. This isn't surprising, since movies and books often have more than one theme. But generally one theme will stand out above the rest as the one that is most important or most obvious. This theme is called the primary theme.

As you read "A Day's Wait," jot down possible themes of the story.

"A Day's Wait" by Ernest Hemingway

Response notes

He came into the room to shut the windows while we were still in bed and I saw he looked ill. He was shivering, his face was white, and he walked slowly as though it ached to move.

"What's the matter, Schatz?"

"I've got a headache."

"You better go back to bed."

"No. I'm all right."

"You go to bed. I'll see you when I'm dressed."

But when I came downstairs he was dressed, sitting by the fire, looking a very sick and miserable boy of nine years. When I put my hand on his forehead I knew he had a fever.

"You go up to bed," I said, "you're sick."

"I'm all right," he said.

When the doctor came he took the boy's temperature.

"What is it?" I asked him.

"One hundred and two."

Downstairs, the doctor left three different medicines in different colored capsules with instructions for giving them. One was to bring down the fever, another a purgative, the third to overcome an acid condition. The germs of influenza can only exist in an acid condition, he explained. He seemed to know all about influenza and said there was nothing to worry about if the fever did not go above one hundred and four degrees. This was a light epidemic of flu and there was no danger if you avoided pneumonia.

Back in the room I wrote the boy's temperature down and made a note of the time to give the various capsules.

"Do you want me to read to you?"

"All right. If you want to," said the boy. His face was very white and there were dark areas under his eyes. He lay still in the bed and seemed very detached from what was going on.

I read aloud from Howard Pyle's *Book of Pirates;* but I could see he was not following what I was reading.

63

"How do you feel, Schatz?" I asked him.

"Just the same, so far," he said.

I sat at the foot of the bed and read to myself while I waited for it to be time to give another capsule. It would have been natural for him to go to sleep, but when I looked up he was looking at the foot of the bed, looking very strangely.

"Why don't you try to go to sleep? I'll wake you up for the medicine."

"I'd rather stay awake."

After a while he said to me, "You don't have to stay in here with me, Papa, if it bothers you."

"It doesn't bother me."

"No, I mean you don't have to stay if it's going to bother you."

I thought perhaps he was a little lightheaded and after giving him the prescribed capsules at eleven o'clock I went out for a while. It was a bright, cold day, the ground covered with a sleet that had frozen so that it seemed as if all the bare trees, the bushes, the cut brush and all the grass and the bare ground had been varnished with ice. I took the young Irish setter for a little walk up the road and along a frozen creek, but it was difficult to stand or walk on the glassy surface and the red dog slipped and slithered and I fell twice, hard, once dropping my gun and having it slide away over the ice.

We flushed a covey of quail under a high clay bank with overhanging brush and I killed two as they went out of sight over the top of the bank. Some of the covey lit in trees, but most of them scattered into brush piles and it was necessary to jump on the ice-coated mounds of brush several times before they would flush. Coming out while you were poised unsteadily on the icy, springy brush they made difficult shooting and I killed two, missed five, and started back pleased to have found a covey close to the house and happy there were so many left to find on another day.

At the house they said the boy had refused to let any one come into the room.

"You can't come in," he said. "You mustn't get what I have."

I went up to him and found him in exactly the position I had left him, white-faced, but with the tops of his cheeks flushed by the fever, staring still, as he had stared, at the foot of the bed.

I took his temperature.

"What is it?"

"Something like a hundred," I said. It was one hundred and two and four tenths.

"A Day's Wait" by Ernest Hemingway

Response notes

"It was a hundred and two," he said.

"Who said so?"

"The doctor."

"Your temperature is all right," I said. "It's nothing to worry about."

"I don't worry," he said, "but I can't keep from thinking."

"Don't think," I said. "Just take it easy."

"I'm taking it easy," he said and looked straight ahead. He was evidently holding tight onto himself about something.

"Take this with water."

"Do you think it will do any good?"

"Of course it will."

I sat down and opened the *Pirate* book and commenced to read, but I could see he was not following, so I stopped.

"About what time do you think I'm going to die?" he asked.

"What?"

"About how long will it be before I die?"

"You aren't going to die. What's the matter with you?"

"Oh, yes, I am. I heard him say a hundred and two."

"People don't die with a fever of one hundred and two. That's a silly way to talk."

"I know they do. At school in France the boys told me you can't live with forty-four degrees. I've got a hundred and two."

He had been waiting to die all day, ever since nine o'clock in the morning.

"You poor Schatz," I said. "Poor old Schatz. It's like miles and kilometers. You aren't going to die. That's a different thermometer. On that thermometer thirty-seven is normal. On this kind it's ninety-eight."

"Are you sure?"

"Absolutely," I said. "It's like miles and kilometers. You know, like how many kilometers we make when we do seventy miles in the car?"

"Oh," he said.

But his gaze at the foot of the bed relaxed slowly. The hold over himself relaxed too, finally, and the next day it was very slack and he cried very easily at little things that were of no importance.

●◆Look back at the possible themes you jotted down as you were reading. List them, adding others that come to mind as you think about the events of the story and what the characters learned.

●◆Look at your list of possible themes. Circle the one that you think is the primary theme. To find it, ask yourself, "What is the most important meaning about life Hemingway conveys in this story? What was he trying to say to readers?" Underline details in the story that support your answer.

Then, in a few sentences, summarize what you think the primary theme is and why it is the most important one.

The primary theme is the most prominent or important theme in a story. To find it, make a mental list of all the themes and choose the one that makes the most sense with the details in the story.

Five
The Secondary Message

Writing seldom, if ever, has only one meaning. So, once you've found the primary theme, you can consider which secondary themes might be valid. Secondary themes are smaller ideas or insights that a writer explores.

➡️ Consider the possible secondary themes below for "A Day's Wait." For each one circle *Agree* (if the statement is a possible secondary theme for the story) or *Disagree* (if it's not a possible theme). Then give proof from the story to support your answer.

1. Parents misunderstand their children.   Agree   Disagree

2. Jumping to conclusions before you know all the facts can have serious consequences.   Agree   Disagree

3. It is irresponsible to leave a child when he is sick.   Agree   Disagree

●◆Begin to plan a story of your own. Think of an event from your childhood that taught you something important. In the space below, plan a story about the event.

Brief description of event

People who were involved

Primary theme

Secondary themes

As you read, look for additional themes beyond the primary one. These secondary themes can add to your understanding of the story.

The Art of Language

To many writers, language is music. A story or poem or novel is a symphony that is composed one note or one word at a time. The poet or writer is the composer who arranges the words into phrases and sentences.

Of course, not all words are musical and not all writing is as complex as a symphony. Some writers, though, have a gift for writing words, stanzas, and paragraphs that seem to soar off the page. What's their secret? What techniques do writers like William Saroyan, Robert Frost, and Eve Merriam use to bring life and vitality to their language? In "The Art of Language" you'll have a chance to find out.

Words are important for how they *sound* and for what they *mean*. They are also important for what they can help you *see*.

A **simile** can help you **visualize** things that the author describes. A simile is a comparison of two unlike things. In a simile, a comparison word (for example, *like* or *as*) is used. Similes can make the language the author uses seem fresher, or more vibrant. Similes can also help readers see familiar things in a whole new way. For example, notice how Henry Wadsworth Longfellow describes a ship's sails:

> A phantom ship, with each mast and spar
> Across the moon like a prison bar. . .
> —from Henry Wadsworth Longfellow's "Paul Revere's Ride"

Longfellow's comparison of the mast to a prison bar helps heighten the feeling of suspense in the poem.

Read "Simile: Willow and Ginkgo" by Eve Merriam. Underline each simile you find.

Response notes

70

Simile: Willow and Ginkgo
Eve Merriam

The willow is like an etching,
Fine-lined against the sky.
The ginkgo is like a crude sketch,
Hardly worthy to be signed.

The willow's music is like a soprano
Delicate and thin.
The ginkgo's tune is like a chorus
With everyone joining in.

The willow is sleek as a velvet-nosed calf;
The ginkgo is leathery as an old bull.
The willow's branches are like silken thread;
The ginkgo's like stubby rough wool.

The willow is like a nymph with streaming hair;
Wherever it grows, there is green and gold and fair.
The willow dips to the water,
Protected and precious, like the king's favorite daughter.

The ginkgo forces its way through gray concrete:
Like a city child, it grows up in the street.
Thrust against the metal sky,
Somehow it survives and even thrives.

My eyes feast upon the willow,
But my heart goes to the ginkgo.

●◆ How does Merriam's use of similes affect your understanding of the differences between the two kinds of trees? Does Merriam's use of similes enhance your understanding or appreciation of the poem? Why or why not?

●◆ Create some similes of your own on the lines below.

The sun is like a copper penny.

My heart beats as fast as

She's more irritated than

The _____ is like

The _____ is as _____ as

●◆ Write a poem of your own using one or more of the similes you've created. Model your poem on "Simile: Willow and Ginkgo."

Writers
use similes to
bring a freshness and
a sense of surprise to
their writing.

Two Metaphor

Metaphors are another option whenever a writer wants to add freshness to his or her writing. A metaphor is like a simile in some ways. It too is a comparison between two unlike things, although no comparison word is used. In creating a metaphor, the writer says one thing *is* another. For example: "A tree is a hand raised toward heaven." Metaphors allow the writer to take us beyond dictionary meanings to see how one thing has characteristics of another.

In "Scaffolding," Seamus Heaney creates an *extended metaphor*—that is, a metaphor that is developed throughout the entire work. Read the poem through several times. Use the response notes to record your impressions.

Scaffolding
Seamus Heaney

Masons, when they start upon a building,
Are careful to test out the scaffolding;

Make sure that planks won't slip at busy points,
Secure all ladders, tighten bolted joints.

And yet all this comes down when the job's done
Showing off walls of sure and solid stone.

So if, my dear, there sometimes seem to be
Old bridges breaking between you and me

Never fear. We may let the scaffolds fall
Confident that we have built our wall.

Response notes

73

●◆ What two things is Heaney comparing in this poem? How are they similar?

●✦ What did you visualize as you were reading "Scaffolding"? Draw a picture of what you "saw."

●✦ Reflect on the building metaphor that Heaney creates in "Scaffolding." Then explain what you think he means by these lines:

Never fear. We may let the scaffolds fall
Confident that we have built our wall.

Metaphors can bring freshness and vitality to a poem. An extended metaphor can help unify the entire poem.

Three
Assonance, Consonance, and Alliteration

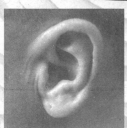

Good writers know that the *sound* of a word can sometimes be as important as the word's meaning. Three techniques that writers use to emphasize the sound of their writing are alliteration, assonance, and consonance.

- **Alliteration** is the repetition of initial consonant sounds in words. For example, look at Seamus Heaney's use of alliteration in "Scaffolding":

So if, my dear, there sometimes seem to be
Old bridges breaking between you and me

- **Assonance** is the repetition of vowel sounds without the repetition of consonants. For example:

And the stars never rise but I see the bright eyes
Of the beautiful Annabel Lee;
And so, all the night-tide; I lie down by the side...

—Edgar Allan Poe, "Annabel Lee"

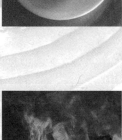

- **Consonance** is the repetition of consonant sounds. The repeated sound can be in the beginning, middle, or end of the word:

"...and high school girls with clear skin smiles..."

—Janis Ian, "At Seventeen"

Authors use alliteration, assonance and consonance for a variety of reasons, including to establish the **mood** (or atmosphere), to reveal meaning, and to unify their work.

Read this poem by Robert Frost. Underline as many examples of assonance and consonance as you can find.

Response notes

Fire and Ice
Robert Frost

Some say the world will end in fire,
Some say in ice.
From what I've tasted of desire
I hold with those who favor fire.
But if I had to perish twice,
I think I know enough of hate
To say that for destruction ice
Is also great
And would suffice.

75

In "Fire and Ice," Frost uses alliteration, assonance, and consonance to create a soothing, sing-song **rhythm,** or beat. You could almost jump rope to the rhythm of this poem—even though the message of the poem is not at all lighthearted. It is the contrast between rhythm and meaning that makes "Fire and Ice" so interesting.

➡ Reread "Fire and Ice." Note examples of assonance and consonance on the Venn diagram below. Use the middle section for the words that belong on both the assonance and the consonance lists.

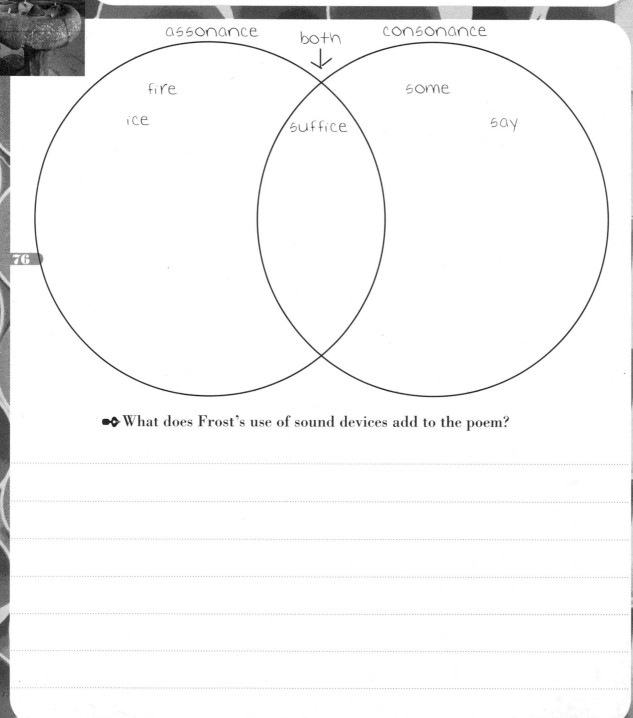

assonance   both ↓   consonance

fire   some

ice   suffice   say

➡ What does Frost's use of sound devices add to the poem?

●◆ Now try using assonance or consonance in your own poetry. Before you begin, make a list of words with repeated vowel sounds and a list of words with repeated consonant sounds.

repeated vowel sounds	repeated consonant sounds

●◆ Use words from your list to write a one-stanza poem that uses alliteration, assonance, consonance, or some combination of the three.

When you read a poem, notice how assonance, consonance, and alliteration are used to enhance meaning.

Four
Setting the Mood

It was a dark and stormy night...

The **mood** of a piece of writing is the atmosphere or climate of the work. A story's mood can be lighthearted and sunny or dark and stormy or anything in-between. Mood can help make the writing interesting and powerful. In some stories, the **setting** of the piece (the time and place) helps set the mood. Word choice, objects, and **details** can also contribute to the mood.

As you read the first part of "Gaston," think carefully about the mood of the story. Make notes in the margin.

"Gaston" by William Saroyan

←Response notes

They were to eat peaches, as planned, after her nap, and now she sat across from the man who would have been a total stranger except that he was in fact her father. They had been together again (although she couldn't quite remember when they had been together before) for almost a hundred years now, or was it only since day before yesterday? Anyhow, they were together again, and he was kind of funny. First, he had the biggest mustache she had ever seen, although to her it was not a mustache at all; it was a lot of red and brown hair under his nose and around the ends of his mouth. Second, he wore a blue-and-white striped jersey instead of a shirt and tie, and no coat. His arms were covered with the same hair, only it was a little lighter and thinner. He wore blue slacks, but no shoes and socks. He was barefoot, and so was she, of course.

He was at home. She was with him in his home in Paris, if you could call it a home. He was very old, especially for a young man—thirty-six, he had told her; and she was six, just up from sleep on a very hot afternoon in August.

That morning, on a little walk in the neighborhood, she had seen peaches in a box outside a small store and she had stopped to look at them, so he had bought a kilo.

Now the peaches were on a large plate on the card table at which they sat. There were seven of them, but one of them was flawed. It looked as good as the others, almost the size of a tennis ball, nice red fading to light green, but where the stem had been there was now a break that went straight down into the heart of the seed.

He placed the biggest and best-looking peach on the small plate in front of the girl and then took the flawed peach and began to remove the skin. When he had half the skin off the

"Gaston" by William Saroyan

Response notes

peach he ate that side, neither of them talking, both of them just being there, and not being excited or anything—no plans, that is.

The man held the half-eaten peach and looked down into the cavity, into the open seed. The girl looked, too.

While they were looking, two feelers poked out from the cavity. They were attached to a kind of brown knob-head, which followed the feelers, and then two large legs took a strong grip on the edge of the cavity and hoisted some of the rest of whatever it was out of the seed, and stopped there a moment, as if to look around.

The man studied the seed dweller, and so, of course, did the girl.

The creature paused only a fraction of a second, and then continued to come out of the seed, to walk down the eaten side of the peach to wherever it was going.

The girl had never seen anything like it—a whole big thing made out of brown color, a knob-head, feelers, and a great many legs. It was very active, too. Almost businesslike, you might say. The man placed the peach back on the plate. The creature moved off the peach onto the surface of the white plate. There it came to a thoughtful stop.

"Who is it?" the girl said.

"Gaston."

"Where does he live?"

"Well, he used to live in this peach seed, but now that the peach has been harvested and sold, and I have eaten half of it, it looks as if he's out of house and home."

"Aren't you going to squash him?"

"No, of course not, why should I?"

"He's a bug. He's ugh."

"Not at all. He's Gaston, the grand *boulevardier*."

"Everybody hollers when a bug comes out of an apple, but you don't holler or anything."

"Of course not. How would we like it if somebody hollered every time we came out of our house?"

"Why should they?"

"Precisely. So why should we holler at Gaston?"

"He's not the same as us."

"Well, not exactly, but he's the same as a lot of other occupants of peach seeds. Now, the poor fellow hasn't got a home, and there he is with all that pure design and handsome form, and nowhere to go."

"Handsome?"

"Gaston is just about the handsomest of his kind I've ever seen."

79

Response notes

"What's he saying?"

"Well, he's a little confused. Now, inside that house of his he had everything in order. Bed here, porch there, etc."

"Show me."

The man picked up the peach, leaving Gaston entirely alone on the white plate. He removed the peeling and ate the rest of the peach.

"Nobody else I know would do that," the girl said. "They'd throw it away."

"I can't imagine why. It's a perfectly good peach." He opened the seed and placed the two sides not far from Gaston. The girl studied the open halves.

"Is that where he lives?"

"It's where he used to live. Gaston is out in the world and on his own now. You can see for yourself how comfortable he was in there. He had everything."

"Now what has he got?"

"Not very much, I'm afraid."

"What's he going to do?"

"What are we going to do?"

"Well, we're not going to squash him, that's one thing we're not going to do," the girl said.

"What are we going to do, then?"

"Put him back?"

"Oh, that house is finished."

"Well, he can't live in our house, can he?"

"Not happily."

"Can he live in our house at all?"

"Well, he could try, I suppose. Don't you want a peach?"

"Only if it's a peach with somebody in the seed."

"Well, see if you can find a peach that has an opening at the top, because if you can, that'll be a peach in which you're likeliest to find somebody."

The girl examined each of the peaches on the big plate.

"They're all shut," she said.

"Well, eat one, then."

"No. I want the same kind that you ate, with somebody in the seed."

"Well, to tell you the truth, the peach I ate would be considered a bad peach, so of course stores don't like to sell them. I was sold that one by mistake, most likely. And so now Gaston is without a home, and we've got six perfect peaches to eat."

"I don't want a perfect peach. I want one with people."

"Well, I'll go out and see if I can find one."

"Where will I go?"

"You'll go with me, unless you'd rather stay. I'll only be five minutes."

THE ART OF LANGUAGE

"Gaston" by William Saroyan

"If the phone rings, what shall I say?"

"I don't think it'll ring, but if it does, say hello and see who it is."

"If it's my mother, what shall I say?"

"Tell her I've gone to get you a bad peach, and anything else you want to tell her."

"If she wants me to go back, what shall I say?"

"Say yes if you want to go back."

"Do you want me to?"

"Of course not, but the important thing is what you want, not what I want."

"Why is that the important thing?"

"Because I want you to be where you want to be."

"I want to be here."

"I'll be right back."

He put on socks and shoes, and a jacket, and went out.

●◆ Describe the setting of "Gaston."

© GREAT SOURCE. ALL RIGHTS RESERVED.

●❖ List at least three words that describe the mood of the story.

●❖ What techniques does Saroyan use to create the mood? How do his setting and word choice affect the mood of the story? Explain.

82

Setting and word choice often enhance a story's mood.

Five Symbolism

Symbolism occurs when a writer uses a person, place, thing, or event to represent something else. Writers often use symbolism in order to turn an abstract concept (something that you can think about but can't see or touch) into something concrete—something that you *can* see or touch. For example, the Statue of Liberty symbolizes the abstract concept of freedom to some people.

Read the second half of Saroyan's piece. Circle any information you find about Gaston and the peach.

"Gaston" (continued) by William Saroyan

Response notes.

She watched Gaston trying to find out what to do next. Gaston wandered around the plate, but everything seemed wrong and he didn't know what to do or where to go.

The telephone rang and her mother said she was sending the chauffeur to pick her up because there was a little party for somebody's daughter who was also six, and then tomorrow they would fly back to New York.

"Let me speak to your father," she said.

"He's gone to get a peach."

"One peach?"

"One with people."

"You haven't been with your father two days and already you sound like him."

"There are peaches with people in them. I know. I saw one of them come out."

"A bug?"

"Not a bug. Gaston."

"Who?"

"Gaston the grand something."

"Somebody else gets a peach with a bug in it and throws it away, but not him. He makes up a lot of foolishness about it."

"It's not foolishness."

"All right, all right, don't get angry at me about a horrible peach bug of some kind."

"Gaston is right here, just outside his broken house, and I'm not angry at you."

"You'll have a lot of fun at the party."

"Okay.

"Are you glad you saw your father?"

"Of course I am."

"Is he funny?"

"Yes."

"Is he crazy?"

"Yes. I mean, no. He doesn't holler when he sees a bug

83

Response notes

crawling out of a peach seed or anything. He just looks at it carefully. But it is just a bug, isn't it really?"

"That's all it is."

"And we'll have to squash it?"

"That's right. I can't wait to see you, darling. These two days have been like two years to me. Goodbye."

The girl watched Gaston on the plate, and she actually didn't like him. He was all ugh, as he had been in the first place. He didn't have a home anymore and he was wandering around on the white plate and he was silly and wrong and ridiculous and useless and all sorts of other things. She cried a little, but only inside, because long ago she had decided she didn't like crying because if you ever started to cry it seemed as if there was so much to cry about you almost couldn't stop, and she didn't like that at all. The open halves of the peach seed were wrong, too. They were ugly or something. They weren't clean.

The man bought a kilo of peaches but found no flawed peaches among them, so he bought another kilo at another store, and this time there were two that were flawed. He hurried back to his flat and let himself in.

His daughter was in her room, in her best dress.

"My mother phoned," she said, "and she's sending the chauffeur for me because there's another birthday party."

"Another?"

"I mean, there's always a lot of them in New York."

"Will the chauffeur bring you back?"

"No. We're flying back to New York tomorrow."

"Oh."

"I liked being in your house."

"I liked having you here."

"Why do you live here?"

"This is my home."

"It's nice, but it's a lot different from our home."

"Yes, I suppose it is."

"It's kind of like Gaston's house."

"Where is Gaston?"

"I squashed him."

"Really? Why?"

"Everybody squashes bugs and worms."

"Oh. Well. I found you a peach."

"I don't want a peach anymore."

"Okay."

He got her dressed, and he was packing her stuff when the chauffeur arrived. He went down the three flights of stairs with his daughter and the chauffeur, and in the street he was about to hug the girl when he decided he had better not. They

84

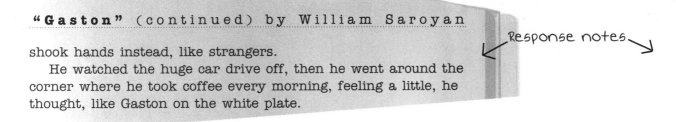

"Gaston" (continued) by William Saroyan

Response notes

shook hands instead, like strangers.

   He watched the huge car drive off, then he went around the corner where he took coffee every morning, feeling a little, he thought, like Gaston on the white plate.

●◆At the end of the story, how are Gaston and the father similar? Use this web to show the characteristics they have in common.

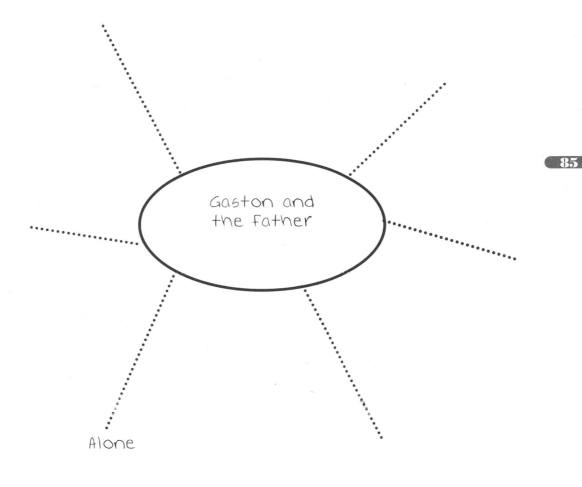

Gaston and the father

Alone

●◆"Gaston symbolizes the father's loneliness." Do you agree or disagree with this statement? Explain in a paragraph or two. If you disagree, explain what you think Gaston and the peach do symbolize. Use lines from the story to help explain your ideas.

Recognizing symbols can help make abstractions more concrete and easier to understand.

The Art of Argument

In literature, argument isn't necessarily about arguing. It's about examining both sides of an issue. Authors of argument want you to look at issues from a new viewpoint—theirs—in order to change your mind or your actions.

The literature of argument surrounds you. You can find it in TV commercials and commentaries, on billboards and bumper stickers, in speeches and sermons, in magazine and newspaper articles. But while some attempts at argument are convincing, others fall flat. As you will discover, there is an art to writing argument—and there is an art to reading it. In the pages that follow, you will sharpen your skills at reading and evaluating written arguments.

One Taking a Position

In written argument, the main idea is called a **thesis statement**. It states the position, or **viewpoint**, with which the author wants readers to agree. Identifying the thesis statement helps you to understand the author's thinking. Sometimes the thesis statement appears in the opening paragraph. Sometimes the author saves it until the end.

A thesis statement may be phrased as a call to action, urging readers to take specific steps, or it may be a plea for readers to change their thinking. A thesis statement may be implied, or unstated; then readers must infer it on their own.

In the letter below, written by the Grand Council Fire of American Indians, the thesis statement appears twice. See if you can identify it as you read.

◁response notes◁

"Memorial and Recommendations of the Grand Council Fire of American Indians"

December 1, 1927

To the mayor of Chicago:

You tell all white men "America First." We believe in that. We are the only ones, truly, that are one hundred percent. We therefore ask you, while you are teaching schoolchildren about America First, teach them truth about the First Americans.

We do not know if school histories are pro-British, but we do know that they are unjust to the life of our people—the American Indian. They call all white victories battles and all Indian victories massacres. The battle with Custer has been taught to schoolchildren as a fearful massacre on our part. We ask that this, as well as other incidents, be told fairly. If the Custer battle was a massacre, what was Wounded Knee?

History books teach that Indians were murderers—is it murder to fight in self-defense? Indians killed white men because white men took their lands, ruined their hunting grounds, burned their forests, destroyed their buffalo. White men penned our people on reservations, then took away the reservations. White men who rise to protect their property are called patriots—Indians who do the same are called murderers.

White men call Indians treacherous—but no mention is made of broken treaties on the part of the white man. White men say that Indians were always fighting. It was only our lack of skill in white man's warfare that led to our defeat. An Indian mother prayed that her boy be a great medicine man rather than a great warrior. It is true that we had our own small battles, but in the main we were peace loving and home loving.

"Memorial and Recommendations of the Grand Council Fire of American Indians"

Response notes

White men called Indians thieves—and yet we lived in frail skin lodges and needed no locks or iron bars. White men call Indians savages. What is civilization? Its marks are a noble religion and philosophy, original arts, stirring music, rich story and legend. We had these. Then we were not savages, but a civilized race.

We made blankets that were beautiful, that the white man with all his machinery has never been able to duplicate. We made baskets that were beautiful. We wove in beads and colored quills designs that were not just decorative motifs but were the outward expression of our very thoughts. We made pottery—pottery that was useful, and beautiful as well. Why not make schoolchildren acquainted with the beautiful handicrafts in which we were skilled? Put in every school Indian blankets, baskets, pottery.

We sang songs that carried in their melodies all the sounds of nature—the running of waters, the sighing of winds, and the calls of the animals. Teach these to your children that they may come to love nature as we love it.

We had our statesmen—and their oratory has never been equaled. Teach the children some of these speeches of our people, remarkable for their brilliant oratory.

We played games—games that brought good health and sound bodies. Why not put these in your schools? We told stories. Why not teach schoolchildren more of the wholesome proverbs and legends of our people? Tell them how we loved all that was beautiful. That we killed game only for food, not for fun. Indians think white men who kill for fun are murderers.

Tell your children of the friendly acts of Indians to the white people who first settled here. Tell them of our leaders and heroes and their deeds. Tell them of Indians such as Black Partridge, Shabbona, and others who many times saved the people of Chicago at great danger to themselves. Put in your history books the Indian's part in the World War. Tell how the Indian fought for a country of which he was not a citizen, for a flag to which he had no claim, and for a people that have treated him unjustly.

The Indian has long been hurt by these unfair books. We ask only that our story be told in fairness. We do not ask you to overlook what we did, but we do ask you to understand it. A true program of America First will give a generous place to the culture and history of the American Indian.

We ask this, Chief, to keep sacred the memory of our people.

Which parts of this letter stand out most in your mind?

A thesis statement calling for action appears near the beginning of the letter. It appears again, in a different form, near the end. In your own words, how would you express this thesis statement?

Do you agree with the thesis statement? Explain your position.

Identifying the thesis statement in a written argument helps readers to understand the author's thinking.

Two **Reasons and Evidence**

A thesis statement should be backed up with reasons, and reasons should be supported by evidence. Good readers examine reasons and evidence carefully. Authors may use several kinds of evidence to support their reasons. Facts, statistics, examples, observations, quotations, and experts' opinions all can provide supporting evidence.

Reread the letter from the Grand Council Fire of American Indians. The authors offer reasons and evidence to back up their statement that textbooks are "unjust to the lives of . . . American Indians."

●◆ Use the chart below to show reasons and evidence that you find. Some examples are done for you.

Reasons	Evidence
Indians are inaccurately portrayed as killers.	Indian victories are called "massacres"; white victories are called "battles."
Indians are inaccurately portrayed as treacherous.	

91

●◆In the letter, the authors stress the contributions of American Indians and suggest that textbooks and lessons in school include these contributions. In your experience, have the changes they recommended occurred? Do you believe they should? Support your answer with reasons and evidence.

Readers can analyze written arguments by identifying the reasons and evidence.

The Other Side

Every issue has two sides. When you read a written argument, ask yourself how—or whether—the author deals with both sides of the issue. Effective writers take both sides into account. They anticipate how readers might object to their views, and they answer those objections.

The newspaper editorial below examines both sides of an issue. Notice how the author deals with possible objections to his views.

"Silencing the Sound of Music" by Dan Rather

As recently as a century or so ago, if you wanted to hear music, you had better play or sing for yourself. If you wanted to hear more than that, you'd better have friends. If you wanted to hear an opera or symphony any time you wanted to, you'd better be a king.

Today, of course, all we need to do is plug in the radio or stereo. One hundred, 200 musicians at our command, any time of the day or night. In the car, at the gym, in the supermarket, anywhere we go, even places we don't want music. We can listen to musicians who aren't even alive anymore, from Patsy Cline to Elvis Presley to Maria Callas.

I have begun to wonder if our easy access to music has made it too easy for us to take music for granted.

Example: School districts feeling the pinch tend to cut music classes first, according to many experts. The reasoning apparently goes like this: Music seems like a frivolity when you compare it to chemistry labs; instruments cost a lot of money (either to the school or to the parents); and, after all, why do you think they call it an "elective"?

Well, this happens to be a subject I know something about. You see, I took music classes in public schools—the Houston Independent School District in Texas. Even then, I was no musical prodigy. They put me in the rhythm band and gave me a wood block to play. I wore it on a cord around my neck and hit it with a little stick.

Other children might have been expected to hit each other with the little stick. Not me. (Well, not often.) I was extremely respectful of my instrument. After all, the wood block is one of the world's oldest musical instruments. Scholars believe the wood block was invented *before* music. And if you needed proof of that, you had only to listen to the way I played.

About the best you could say for my performance was this: I very seldom played off-key.

Response notes

93

"Silencing the Sound of Music" by Dan Rather

I was also—don't ask how or why—assistant conductor of the Alexander Hamilton Elementary School band. To this day I can still conduct about three songs, just in case I'm at the concert hall one night and there's an emergency and somebody shouts: "Is there a conductor in the house?"

In all honesty, those little music classes didn't turn me into a musician—you'd need a *magician* to do that. But those classes did give me an appreciation of music.

• Music is difficult. It requires work and thought and sweat and inspiration. I haven't taken it for granted since.

• Music is exciting. It is truly thrilling to be sitting in a group of musicians when you are all playing (more or less) the same piece of music. You are part of a great, powerful, vibrant entity. And nothing beats the feeling you get when you've practiced a difficult section over and over, and finally get it right. (Yes, even on the wood block.)

And you think *you're* excited when you get that song right: Imagine how your *mother* feels. You can see it in her face: relief and pride. Big pride.

• Music is important. It says things your heart can't say any other way, and in a language everyone speaks. Music crosses borders, turns smiles to frowns, and vice versa.

These observations are shared with a hope: that, when schools cut back on music classes, they really think about what they're doing—and don't take music for granted.

How important is music in your life? Describe when you listen to it or play it, and explain why.

Dan Rather acknowledges the opposition—the other side of the issue—with the sentence that begins "The reasoning apparently goes like this . . . " (paragraph 4). Near the end of his editorial, he outlines his own reasoning, marking each reason with a bullet (•). In your opinion, does Rather respond effectively to the opposition? Explain your response.

95

Use the space below to create a bumper sticker that would express your views on the issue that Dan Rather examines.

An effective argument deals with both sides of an issue.

Four
Facts and Opinions

Good readers know the difference between facts and opinions. A **fact** is a statement that can be proven. An **opinion** is one person's view; it can't be proven.

> ### Opinion
> Athens was the best city-state in ancient Greece.
> (Who says? Who defines "best"?)

> ### Fact
> Athens flourished as a city-state between 700 and 400 B.C.
> (This fact could be proven by checking an encyclopedia or a history book.)

Facts and opinions both have valid uses in argumentative writing. An opinion well supported with facts can be convincing. The opinion of an expert can often carry as much weight as a fact. A responsible author, however, is careful not to present his or her opinions as if they were facts.

In the essay below, Andy Rooney uses both facts and opinions to make his point. First read his essay. Then go back and mark facts with an *F* and opinions with an *O*.

"America the Not-so-Beautiful" by Andy Rooney

Response notes

Next to saving stuff I don't need, the thing I like to do best is throw it away. My idea of a good time is to load up the back of the car with junk on a Saturday morning and take it to the dump. There's something satisfying about discarding almost anything.

Throwing things out is the American way. We don't know how to fix anything, and anyone who does know how is too busy to come, so we throw it away and buy a new one. Our economy depends on us doing that. The trouble with throwing things away is, there is no "away" left.

Sometime around the year 500 B.C., the Greeks in Athens passed a law prohibiting people from throwing their garbage in the street. This Greek law was the first recognition by civilized people that throwing things away was a problem. Now, as the population explodes and people take up more room on earth, there's less room for everything else.

The more civilized a country is, the worse the trash problem is. Poor countries don't have the same problem because they don't have much to discard. Prosperity in the United States is based on using things up as fast as we can, throwing away what's left, and buying new ones.

We've been doing that for so many years that (1) we've run

"America the Not-so-Beautiful" by Andy Rooney

Response notes

out of places to throw things because houses have been built where the dump was and (2) some of the things we're throwing away are poisoning the earth and will eventually poison all of us and all living things.

Ten years ago most people thought nothing of dumping an old bottle of weed or insect killer in a pile of dirt in the back yard or down the drain in the street, just to get rid of it. The big companies in America had the same feeling, on a bigger scale. For years the chemical companies dumped their poisonous wastes in the rivers behind the mills, or they put it in fifty-gallon drums in the vacant lots, with all the old, rusting machinery in it, up behind the plants. The drums rusted out in ten years and dumped their poison into the ground. It rained, the poisons seeped into the underground streams and poisoned everything for miles around. Some of the manufacturers who did this weren't even evil. They were dumb and irresponsible. Others were evil because they knew how dangerous it was but didn't want to spend the money to do it right.

The problem is staggering. I often think of it when I go in a hardware store or a Sears, Roebuck and see shelves full of poison. You know that, one way or another, it's all going to end up in the earth or in our rivers and lakes.

I have two pint bottles of insecticide with 5 percent DDT in them in my own garage that I don't know what to do with. I bought them years ago when I didn't realize how bad they were. Now I'm stuck with them.

The people of the city of New York throw away nine times their weight in garbage and junk every year. Assuming other cities come close to that, how long will it be before we trash the whole earth?

Of all household waste, 30 percent of the weight and 50 percent of the volume is the packaging that stuff comes in.

Not only that, but Americans spend more for the packaging of food than all our farmers together make in income growing it. That's some statistic.

Trash collectors are a lot more independent than they used to be because we've got more trash than they've got places to put it. They have their own schedules and their own holidays. Some cities try to get in good with their trash collectors or garbage men by calling them "sanitation engineers." Anything just so long as they pick it up and take it away.

We often call the dump "the landfill" now, too. I never understood why land has to be filled, but that's what it's called. If you're a little valley just outside town, you have to be careful or first thing you know you'll be getting "filled."

If 5 billion people had been living on earth for the past

"America the Not-so-Beautiful" by Andy Rooney

thousand years as they have been in the past year, the planet would be nothing but one giant landfill, and we'd have turned America the beautiful into one huge landfill.

The best solution may be for all of us to pack up, board a spaceship, and move out. If Mars is habitable, everyone on Earth can abandon this planet we've trashed, move to Mars, and start trashing that. It'll buy us some time.

●◆ How serious do you consider the problems that Andy Rooney describes? Explain your views.

●◆ Two facts from Rooney's essay are listed below. Add one more fact that you found as you read. Then write how you might check each fact.

Fact	Possible way to check
"The people of the city of New York throw away nine times their weight in garbage and junk every year."	
"Of all household waste, 30 percent of the weight and 50 percent of the volume is the packaging that stuff comes in."	

In Rooney's opinion, some manufacturers who once polluted groundwater with poisons were "evil," and some were not. In a short paragraph, explain how he supports his opinions and whether or not he has convinced you.

99

Recognizing
facts and opinions helps
readers evaluate written

Authors of argument appeal to readers' feelings, as well as to reason. Examining these appeals can help you evaluate an argument. Humor is one kind of appeal to feelings. The use of emotion-laden words is another. Authors who refer to basic values, such as kindness, justice, responsibility, freedom, or patriotism, are also appealing to readers' feelings.

Emotion-laden words	
Pro	**Con**
Senator X is <u>firm</u>.	Senator X is <u>stubborn</u>.
Senator X dresses <u>casually</u>.	Senator X dresses <u>sloppily</u>.
Appeal to basic values	
Pro	**Con**
Senator X <u>supports individual freedom</u>.	Senator X wants to <u>undermine our national government</u>.

In contrast, logical thinking is an appeal to reason. Most appeals to reason feature points or conclusions backed up with examples, **facts**, statistics, or other forms of evidence. Appeals to reason must make sense. If they are based on inaccurate facts or on too little evidence, they may not be valid.

On the chart below, check off the kinds of appeals you find in each argument in this unit. Compare your findings with those of classmates, and be ready to show examples of the kinds of appeals you checked.

Appeals to reason:	"Memorial and Recommendations ..."	"Silencing the Sound of Music"	"America the Not-so-Beautiful"
statistics			
examples			
facts			
Appeals to feelings:			
emotional language			
humor			
mention of basic values			

❧❖ Which of these three arguments do you find most convincing? Why? Did the argument appeal more to your reason or your feelings? How did these appeals affect your evaluation? Explain in a paragraph.

●◆Write a brief argument of your own. In it, support or refute views from a selection in this unit. Take opposing opinions into account. Use appeals to feelings and to reason, and be sure your reasoning makes sense.

102

Readers
can evaluate an argument by
examining its appeals to reason
and to emotion.

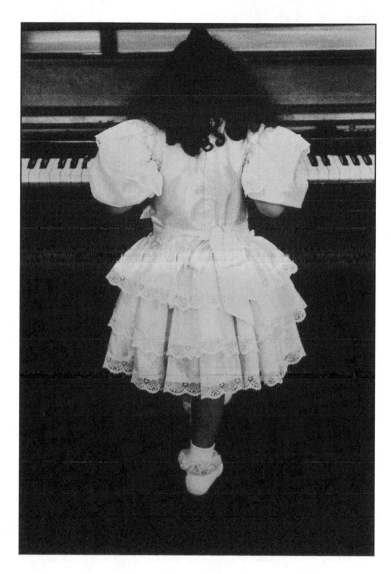

Focus on the Writer: Cynthia Rylant

On the outside looking in—that's how Cynthia Rylant felt at times during her childhood. Today, as an author, she often explores the perspectives of sensitive outsiders. Reading her novels, stories, and poems, you may find yourself looking through the eyes of an eccentric or a dreamer, a lover or a loner, or another character who doesn't always fit in with the crowd. Reading her nonfiction, you can find her reflections on the gift of sensitivity and the challenges that it brings.

All authors have unique perspectives that are shaped by their life experiences. Through reading, you can be enriched by these perspectives. "You never really know what surprises life will pull," observes Cynthia Rylant. "You may think you can see yourself at twenty-five or thirty-five or sixty-five, but the universe has more imagination than you have. And it's going to surprise you."

Characters in Perspective

Story characters can be windows to an author's perspective. Characters may illustrate ideas that the author considers important, or they may give you clues to the author's likes, dislikes, or memories. Some of Cynthia Rylant's characters reflect the traits of people she knew when she was growing up in the mountains of West Virginia.

Rylant's novel *Missing May* is told from the perspective of a twelve-year-old girl named Summer. In this excerpt, Summer recalls the day, six years earlier, when she went to live with her Aunt May and Uncle Ob. Her parents had recently died. As you read, try to picture May, Ob, and Summer.

Response Notes

104

from *Missing May* by Cynthia Rylant

Home was, still is, a rusty old trailer stuck on the face of a mountain in Deep Water, in the heart of Fayette County. It looked to me, the first time, like a toy that God had been playing with and accidentally dropped out of heaven. Down and down and down it came and landed, thunk, on this mountain, sort of cockeyed and shaky and grateful to be all in one piece. Well, sort of one piece. Not counting that part in the back where the aluminum's peeling off, or the one missing window, or the front steps that are sinking.

That first night in it with Ob and May was as close to paradise as I may ever come in my life. Paradise because these two old people—who never dreamed they'd be bringing a little girl back from their visit with the relatives in Ohio—started, from the minute we pulled up in Ob's old Valiant, to turn their rusty, falling-down place into a house just meant for a child. May started talking about where they'd hang the swing as soon as she hoisted herself out of the front seat (May was a big woman), and Ob was designing a tree house in his head before he even got the car shut off. I was still so sick to my stomach from traveling all those curvy West Virginia roads that all I could do was swallow and nod, swallow and nod. Try to smile without puking.

But when we got inside the trailer, it became plain to me at once that they didn't need to do any great changing to make a little girl happy. First thing I saw when May switched on the light were those shelves and shelves—seemed every wall was covered with them—of whirligigs. I knew what they were right off even though they weren't like any whirligigs I'd ever seen. Back in Ohio people had them hooked to their fences or stuck out in their gardens to scare off the birds. And they'd be mostly the same everywhere: a roadrunner whose legs spun in

from *Missing May* by Cynthia Rylant

the wind, or maybe a chicken or a duck. Cartoon characters were popular—Garfield was in a lot of gardens with his arms whirling like crazy in the breeze.

I'd seen plenty of whirligigs, but never any like Ob's. Ob was an artist—I could tell that the minute I saw them—though *artist* isn't the word I could have used back then, so young. None of Ob's whirligigs were farm animals or cartoon characters. They were *The Mysteries*. That's what Ob told me, and I knew just what he was talking about. One whirligig was meant to be a thunderstorm and it was so like one, black and gray, beautiful and frightening. Another was Ob's idea of heaven, and I thought his angels just might come off that thing and fly around that house trailer any minute, so golden and light were they. There was Fire and Love and Dreams and Death. Even one called May, which had more little spinning parts than any of the rest of the whirligigs and these parts all white—her spirit, he said.

●◆ In this selection, Summer is an outsider, coming to May and Ob's home for the first time. List some of the things that she notices about May, Ob, and their trailer. After each item on your list, write Summer's feelings about it. An example is done for you.

What Summer Notices	Summer's Feelings About It
beat-up old trailer	reminds her of a toy—I think she likes it

●◆ Based on your list, what qualities in May and Ob do you think Summer values most? Explain.

●◆ What insights does this excerpt (and your list) give you into Rylant's perspective?

Looking
carefully at what story
characters say and think can help
you understand an author's
perspective.

Two
Perspective and Style

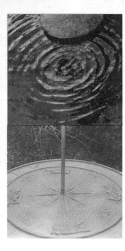

An author's **style**—the unique way that he or she uses language—can also reflect perspective. Style is made up of numerous elements, including:

- the words that the writer chooses
- the rhythms and patterns of the writer's sentences
- the metaphors and similes that the writer creates

Cynthia Rylant chooses colorful, informal words such as *cockeyed, thunk,* and *whirling.* Her sentences follow informal speech patterns; she even includes some fragments, as people do when talking with friends or family. Her **similes** (comparisons using the words *like* or *as*) are unusually detailed. For example, she compares May and Ob's trailer not just to a toy, but to a toy "dropped out of heaven." Her informal, realistic style eases her readers into the world and minds of her characters.

As you read the next excerpt from *Missing May*, circle words and phrases that you find vivid or striking. Underline any similes that you notice.

from ***Missing May*** by Cynthia Rylant

Response notes

107

And as if the whirligigs weren't enough, May turned me to the kitchen, where she pulled open all the cabinet doors, plus the refrigerator, and she said, "Summer, whatever you like you can have and whatever you like that isn't here Uncle Ob will go down to Ellet's Grocery and get you. We want you to eat, honey."

Back in Ohio, where I'd been treated like a homework assignment somebody was always having to do, eating was never a joy of any kind. Every house I had ever lived in was so particular about its food, and especially when the food involved me. There's no good way to explain this. But I felt like one of those little mice who has to figure out the right button to push before its food will drop down into the cup. Caged and begging. That's how I felt sometimes.

My eyes went over May's wildly colorful cabinets, and I was free again. I saw Oreos and Ruffles and big bags of Snickers. Those little cardboard boxes of juice that I had always, just once, wanted to try. I saw fat bags of marshmallows and cans of SpaghettiOs and a little plastic bear full of honey. There were real glass bottles of Coke looking cold as ice in the refrigerator and a great big half of a watermelon taking up space. And, best of all, a carton of real chocolate milk that said Hershey's.

Whirligigs of Fire and Dreams, glistening Coke bottles and chocolate milk cartons to greet me. I was six years old and I had come home.

●◆Use the chart below to examine Cynthia Rylant's writing style in *Missing May*. In the first column, list elements of Rylant's style. In the second column, provide examples from the excerpts.

Elements of Rylant's Style	Examples from Missing May
Colorful, informal words	cockeyed, thunk, whirling
Informal speech patterns	

●◆How does Rylant's style help or hinder your ability to see the world from Summer's perspective? Explain.

Looking at style—an author's unique way of using language—can help you understand more about the author's perspective.

108

Three

Perspective and Theme

A writer's **themes** provide insights into his or her perspective. A **theme** is a generalization or statement about life, the world, or human nature. To find the theme of a story or poem, you can ask yourself what readers might learn from the characters' experiences. Through her characters, Cynthia Rylant often explores people's inner realities—which can be very different from what shows on the outside.

In *The Soda Jerk*, one of Rylant's volumes of poetry, the speaker in the poems is a boy working at a soda fountain in a small town. As you read the poem, jot down your thoughts about possible themes.

Sandy Jane Meador
Cynthia Rylant

Sandy Jane Meador
is a popular girl
and when she comes in
she is very nice
and she smiles a lot
and she never lets there be

a hole

in the conversation;
she never lets there be
one of those
a^{w}k^{w}a^{r}d m^{o}m^{e}n^{t}s
in life. . . .

And you are very nice
and you smile a lot
and you fill up
all the conversation holes
as fast as she does,
so Sandy Jane
will leave
feeling good about
how it all went
and thinking
how nice you are
and believing
how nice she is,
and you are so tired
from all that work
keeping the popular girl
popular.
And typical of the jerk you are,
you hope she liked you.

Response notes

●◆In your own words, write in the thought balloons what the speaker in the poem thinks and feels as he talks with Sandy Jane.

●◆ In the second to last line of the poem, the speaker refers to himself as a "jerk." Do you agree with his assessment of himself? Explain why or why not.

●◆ What does this poem say to you about inner reality vs. outward appearances? Explore how this theme connects to Rylant's perspective of "an outsider looking in."

Exploring the themes of stories and poems can help you gain insights into an author's perspective.

Perspective in Autobiography

In **autobiography**, writers tell about their own lives. An autobiography is a self-portrait, and it helps readers form their own mental portraits of the writer. In the events, people, and experiences that shaped the writer, readers can often find keys to the writer's perspective.

Cynthia Rylant writes about her childhood and teen years in *But I'll Be Back Again*, a collection of autobiographical essays. She and her mother lived in the small town of Beaver, West Virginia.

Response notes

from *But I'll Be Back Again* by Cynthia Rylant

I think my idea of heaven when I was a kid was Christy Sanders' home. She lived in a new brick house with carpeting in it and a bar in the kitchen you could eat on and a picture window in the living room. Her dad wore suits and her mother was queen of the P.T.A. Christy's house always smelled like those chocolate-covered marshmallow cookies you can get at the grocery. Everything in it was new and it matched and it worked.

In the apartment my mother and I shared, there were old gas heaters you had to light with a match and which threatened to blow you up every time you did. We didn't have carpet. We had old green and brown linoleum with cigarette burns in it. Every morning there would be at least one spider in the bathtub, and it would take every ounce of nerve I had to look in and check. Once a really big spider crawled out from under our old couch and I was too scared to step on him; instead I dropped a Sears catalog on his head and left it there for a week, just to make sure he was dead.

If you looked out our front window you would have seen Todd's warehouse and junkyard. It was a long metal building enclosed by a high chain-link fence, and on the outside were rusting barrels and parts of bulldozers and all manner of rotten equipment. There was some talk that the ghost of Mr. Todd's old father walked around that warehouse at night, but I was too worried about spiders in my bathtub to give it much thought.

Wanting Christy Sanders' brick house was just a symptom of the overall desire I had for better things. I read a lot of magazines, and I wanted to live in houses with yellow drapes and backyard pools. I was ashamed of where I lived and felt the world would judge me unworthy because of it. I wouldn't even go to the library in the nearby city because I felt so unequal to city kids. Consequently, I lived on comic books for most of my childhood, until I moved into drugstore paperback romances as a teenager.

from *But I'll Be Back Again* by Cynthia Rylant

Response notes

As long as I stayed in Beaver, I felt I was somebody important. I felt smart and pretty and fun. But as soon as I left town to go anywhere else, my sense of being somebody special evaporated into nothing and I became dull and ugly and poor.

●◆ In what ways did Rylant feel like an outsider as a teenager? Which details from *But I'll Be Back Again* help you understand her feelings?

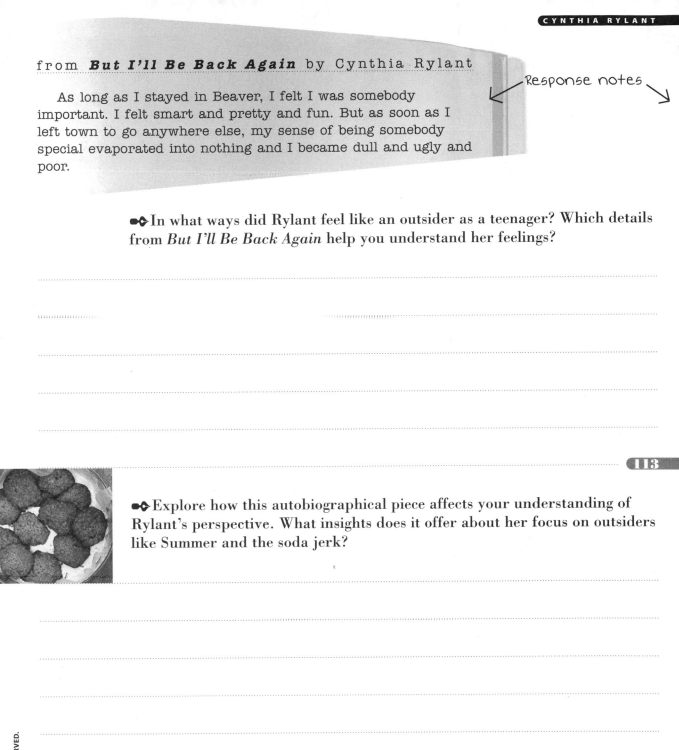

●◆ Explore how this autobiographical piece affects your understanding of Rylant's perspective. What insights does it offer about her focus on outsiders like Summer and the soda jerk?

Knowing about an author's background can help you better understand the author's perspective.

Sometimes authors come right out and tell you about their perspective. They may do this by explaining their views and ideas, or by reflecting on the effects that events or people have on them. Cynthia Rylant's autobiographical writing includes her reflections on her experiences.

In the following excerpt, Rylant tells about a key event of her junior-high years. Though the event itself may seem small, its effect on her is great. Notice how she helps readers see it from her perspective.

114

from **But I'll Be Back Again** by Cynthia Rylant

Response notes

One year, the New Orleans Symphony Orchestra came to play in our junior high school gymnasium. What that orchestra was doing in my little town I cannot imagine, for surely they were all fresh out of London and New York and Los Angeles and didn't need any extra publicity in Beaver, West Virginia.

But the visit of that orchestra was something I have never forgotten. I was not familiar with any real sort of culture. No one I knew played classical records. I had never been to a museum of any kind. In fact, it would not be until I went to college in Charleston, West Virginia, that I set foot in a library or art museum.

The New Orleans Symphony was for me like a visit from God Himself, so full of awe and humility was I. We sat on the hard bleachers our bottoms usually warmed for junior varsity games, and we watched these elegant people who seemed long and fluid like birds play their marvelous instruments. Their music bounced off the blue and gold picture of our school tiger on the wall and the time clock and the heavy velvet curtains we used for school plays, and the gym was transformed into a place of wonder for me.

The conductor was a slender, serious man with a large nose and a lot of dark hair swept back from his forehead. I watched him and I wanted to live in his pink house in New Orleans, surrounded by maids carrying iced tea and peanuts, sleeping each night in a white canopy bed, greeting at the door of our home such notable musicians as Elvis Presley, Paul McCartney, and The Monkees.

Watching the conductor and his beautiful orchestra, I felt something in me that wanted more than I had. Wanted to walk among musicians and artists and writers. Wanted a life beyond Saturdays at G. C. Murphy's department store and Sundays with the Baptist Youth Fellowship.

from *But I'll Be Back Again* by Cynthia Rylant

I wanted to be someone else, and that turned out to be the worst curse and the best gift of my life. I would finish out my childhood forgetting who I really was and what I really thought, and I would listen to other people and repeat their ideas instead of finding my own. That was the curse. The gift was that I would be willing to try to write books when I grew up.

Response notes

●◆ Reread the last paragraph. What do you think about Rylant's "worst curse and the best gift" of her life?

115

●◆In a journal entry, write about an experience that helped to shape your perspective. Discuss your thoughts and feelings at the time. Include your reflections on the experience, as Rylant does.

When you read autobiographies, look for reflections that might explain the author's perspective.

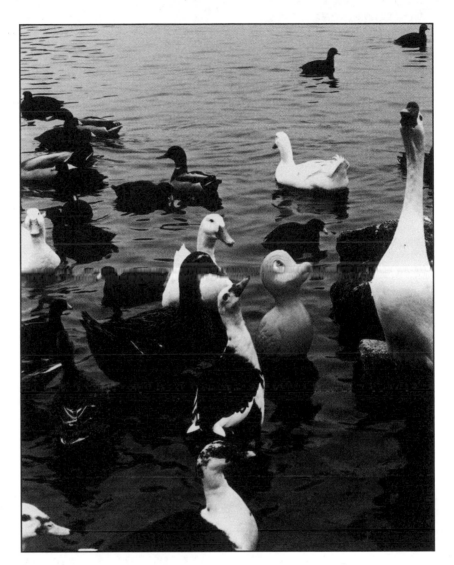

The Reader's Response

How do you respond as a reader? Do you give your opinions ("This was interesting") and make inferences ("I think the author is talking about love here")? Do you keep track of what happens in a story, why it happens, when it happens, and whom it happens to? Do you reread passages that you find interesting or puzzling? These are all ways of responding to what you read.

In this unit, you'll learn some ways to sharpen your ability to respond to literature. You'll also learn how to build one response upon another. As you work your way through each selection, ask yourself: "What is my initial response to this article or poem or story?" and "How can I build upon my first response so that I get more out of what I read?"

One Factual Response

When you read, you respond to the **facts**—the things that are known to be true. Most of the time you are not even conscious of making a factual response. But much of the time you are reading, you are searching for answers to such factual questions as: *who, what, where, when,* and *how.*

Read this excerpt from Eleanor Roosevelt's autobiography. As you read, look for important facts about Eleanor. Circle details that relate to *who, what, where, when,* and *how.*

response notes

from *The Autobiography of Eleanor Roosevelt*
by Eleanor Roosevelt

In the beginning, because I felt, as only a young girl can feel it, all the pain of being an ugly duckling, I was not only timid, I was afraid. Afraid of almost everything, I think: of mice, of the dark, of imaginary dangers, of my own inadequacy. My chief objective, as a girl, was to do my duty. This had been drilled into me as far back as I could remember. Not my duty as I saw it, but my duty as laid down for me by other people. It never occurred to me to revolt. Anyhow, my one overwhelming need in those days was to be approved, to be loved, and I did whatever was required of me, hoping it would bring me nearer to the approval and love I so much wanted.

As a young woman, my sense of duty remained as strict and rigid as it had been when I was a girl, but it had changed its focus. My husband and my children became the center of my life and their needs were my new duty. I am afraid now that I approached this new obligation much as I had my childhood duties. I was still timid, still afraid of doing something wrong, of making mistakes, of not living up to the standards required by my mother-in-law, of failing to do what was expected of me.

As a result, I was so hidebound by duty that I became too critical, too much of a disciplinarian. I was so concerned with bringing up my children properly that I was not wise enough just to love them. Now, looking back, I think I would rather spoil a child a little and have more fun out of it.

It was not until I reached middle age that I had the courage to develop interests of my own, outside of my duties to my family. In the beginning, it seems to me now, I had no goal beyond the interests themselves, in learning about people and conditions and the world outside our own United States. Almost at once I began to discover that interest leads to interest, knowledge leads to more knowledge, the capacity for understanding grows with the effort to understand.

from *The Autobiography of Eleanor Roosevelt*
by Eleanor Roosevelt

From that time on, though I have had many problems, though I have known the grief and the loneliness that are the lot of most human beings, though I have had to make and still have to make endless adjustments, I have never been bored, never found the days long enough for the range of activities with which I wanted to fill them. And, having learned to stare down fear, I long ago reached the point where there is no living person whom I fear, and few challenges that I am not willing to face.

What do you think of Eleanor Roosevelt? Explain.

....

....

....

....

....

....

....

....

Now take a moment to collect the facts you learned about Eleanor Roosevelt.

Who is she?

....

What is she describing?

....

When is she writing?

....

How did she change?

....

➦ Write a brief profile of Eleanor Roosevelt. Use the facts you listed on the previous page in addition to the notes you made while reading the essay to help you with your description.

One way that readers respond is by understanding the who, what, where, when, and how of what they read.

Two Interpretive Response

When you *interpret* what you read, you move beyond the factual (or literal) level and begin to think about the story's underlying meaning. Interpreting involves moving from the words on the page to what those words mean.

Interpreting a poem or story is all about asking "why" questions. For example: Why does a character say what he says or do what he does? Why is the **tone** or **mood** of the story so dark?

Read "Because I could not stop for Death." Note your "why" questions in the margins.

Because I could not stop for Death
Emily Dickinson

Because I could not stop for Death—
He kindly stopped for me—
The Carriage held but just Ourselves—
And Immortality.

We slowly drove—He knew no haste
And I had put away
My labor and my leisure too,
For His Civility—

We passed the School, where Children strove
At Recess—in the Ring—
We passed the Fields of Gazing Grain—
We passed the Setting Sun—

Or rather—He passed Us—
The Dews drew quivering and chill—
For only Gossamer, my Gown—
My Tippet—only Tulle—

We paused before a House that seemed
A Swelling of the Ground—
The Roof was scarcely visible—
The Cornice—in the Ground—

Since then—'tis Centuries—and yet
Feels shorter than the Day
I first surmised the Horses' Heads
Were toward Eternity—

Response notes

121

There is so much that Dickinson does not tell us in this poem. She does not name the speaker, for example, or tell us the cause of death. She does not explain how the speaker feels about dying or even how he or she died. Dickinson leaves all of that up to us and our ability to find hidden meaning. Look at these lines from the poem. Paraphrase what you think each line means.

Lines from the poem	My paraphrase of what the poet is saying	Questions, comments, ideas
Because I could not stop for Death—	The speaker had not prepared for death.	What's with the unusual capitalization and punctuation?
He kindly stopped for me—		
The Carriage held but just Ourselves—		
The Dews drew quivering and chill—		
Since then—'tis Centuries—and yet		

122

●◆Now write four "why" questions about Dickinson's poem. Use your chart and the notes you made while reading the poem to help you write your questions. Then exchange *Daybooks* with a partner. Answer each other's questions as best you can.

1.

Answer:

2.

Answer:

3.

Answer:

4.

Answer:

When you interpret, you make reasonable guesses about a selection's meaning.

Three

Supporting Your Interpretation

When you interpret a story or poem, you think about its underlying meaning. You should also think about how you might support each interpretation you make with evidence from the selection.

To support an interpretation, find a word or phrase that helps explain your views. For example, look at how this reader supports her interpretation of Dickinson's poem:

interpretation: The speaker was unprepared for death.

too busy (support)

Because I could not stop for Death—
He kindly stopped for me—
The Carriage held but just Ourselves—
And Immortality.

We slowly drove—He knew no haste
And I had put away
My labor and my leisure too,
For His Civility—

We passed the School, where Children strove
At Recess—in the Ring—
We passed the Fields of Gazing Grain—
We passed the Setting Sun—

Or rather—He passed Us—
The Dews drew quivering and chill—
For only Gossamer, my Gown—
My Tippet—only Tulle—

wrong dress (support)

not sure where they're going (support)

We paused before a House that seemed
A Swelling of the Ground—
The Roof was scarcely visible—
The Cornice—in the Ground—

Since then—'tis Centuries—and yet
Feels shorter than the Day
I first surmised the Horses' Heads
Were toward Eternity—

124

MELVILLE

•❖Now return to Dickinson's poem and find four or five pieces of support for this interpretation:

<u>Dickinson thinks death will come slowly and peacefully.</u>

•

•

•

•

•

125

•❖Write a paragraph in which you explain why you agree or disagree with Dickinson's view of death. Be sure to support your view.

Good readers build an interpretation by finding words or phrases from a selection to support their views.

Four Evaluative Response

When you evaluate a story, you make a judgment about what you have read. Was the selection interesting? Was it well written? Was it worth reading? In addition to evaluating the selection as a whole, you can also evaluate the characters, the theme, the setting, and so on.

Read the first part of William Sleator's "The Elevator." As you read, jot down your responses in the margins.

Response notes

"The Elevator" by William Sleator

It was an old building with an old elevator—a very small elevator, with a maximum capacity of three people. Martin, a thin twelve-year-old, felt nervous in it from the first day he and his father moved into the apartment. Of course he was always uncomfortable in elevators, afraid that they would fall, but there was something especially unpleasant about this one. Perhaps its baleful atmosphere was due to the light from the single fluorescent ceiling strip, bleak and dim on the dirty brown walls. Perhaps the problem was the door, which never stayed open quite long enough, and slammed shut with such ominous, clanging finality. Perhaps it was the way the mechanism shuddered in a kind of exhaustion each time it left a floor, as though it might never reach the next one. Maybe it was simply the dimensions of the contraption that bothered him, so small that it felt uncomfortably crowded even when there was only one other person in it.

Coming home from school the day after they moved in, Martin tried the stairs. But they were almost as bad, windowless, shadowy, with several dark landings where the light bulbs had burned out. His footsteps echoed behind him like slaps on the cement, as though there was another person climbing, getting closer. By the time he reached the seventeenth floor, which seemed to take forever, he was winded and gasping.

His father, who worked at home, wanted to know why he was so out of breath. "But why didn't you take the elevator?" he asked, frowning at Martin when he explained about the stairs. Not only are you skinny and weak and bad at sports, his expression seemed to say, but you're also a coward. After that, Martin forced himself to take the elevator. He would have to get used to it, he told himself, just the way he got used to being bullied at school, and always picked last when they chose teams. The elevator was an undeniable fact of life.

"The Elevator" by William Sleator

He didn't get used to it. He remained tense in the trembling little box, his eyes fixed on the numbers over the door that blinked on and off so haltingly, as if at any moment they might simply give up. Sometimes he forced himself to look away from them, to the Emergency Stop button, or the red Alarm button. What would happen if he pushed one of them? Would a bell ring? Would the elevator stop between floors? And if it did, how would they get him out?

That was what he hated about being alone on the thing—the fear of being trapped there for hours by himself. But it wasn't much better when there were other passengers. He felt too close to any other rider, too intimate. And he was always very conscious of the effort people made not to look at one another, staring fixedly at nothing. Being short, in this one situation, was an advantage, since his face was below the eye level of adults, and after a brief glance they ignored him.

Until the morning the elevator stopped at the fourteenth floor, and the fat lady got on. She wore a threadbare green coat that ballooned around her; her ankles bulged above dirty sneakers. As she waddled into the elevator, Martin was sure he felt it sink under her weight. She was so big that she filled the cubicle; her coat brushed against him, and he had to squeeze into the corner to make room for her—there certainly wouldn't have been room for another passenger. The door slammed quickly behind her. And then, unlike everyone else, she did not stand facing the door. She stood with her back to the door, wheezing, staring directly at Martin.

For a moment he met her gaze. Her features seemed very small, squashed together by the loose, fleshy mounds of her cheeks. She had no chin, only a great swollen mass of neck, barely contained by the collar of her coat. Her sparse red hair was pinned back by a plastic barrette. And her blue eyes, though tiny, were sharp and penetrating, boring into Martin's face.

Abruptly he looked away from her to the numbers over the door. She didn't turn around. Was she still looking at him? His eyes slipped back to hers, then quickly away. She *was* still watching him. He wanted to close his eyes; he wanted to turn around and stare into the corner, but how could he? The elevator creaked down to twelve, down to eleven. Martin looked at his watch; he looked at the numbers again. They weren't even down to nine yet. And then, against his will, his eyes slipped back to her face. She was still watching him. Her nose tilted up; there was a large space between her nostrils and her upper lip, giving her a piggish look. He looked away again,

127

Response notes

clenching his teeth, fighting the impulse to squeeze his eyes shut against her.

She had to be crazy. Why else would she stare at him this way? What was she going to do next?

She did nothing. She only watched him, breathing audibly, until the elevator reached the first floor at last. Martin would have rushed past her to get out, but there was no room. He could only wait as she turned—reluctantly, it seemed to him—and moved so slowly out into the lobby. And then he ran. He didn't care what she thought. He ran past her, outside into the fresh air, and he ran almost all the way to school. He had never felt such relief in his life.

He thought about her all day. Did she live in the building? He had never seen her before, and the building wasn't very big—only four apartments on each floor. It seemed likely that she didn't live there, and had only been visiting somebody.

But if she were only visiting somebody, why was she leaving the building at seven thirty in the morning? People didn't make visits at that time of day. Did that mean she *did* live in the building? If so, it was likely—it was a certainty—that sometime he would be riding with her on the elevator again.

128

●❖ What do you think of Sleator's story so far?

....

....

....

....

....

●❖ Now complete this sentence by inserting adjectives in the blanks.

The first half of "The Elevator" is _____ and _____.
Explain your opinion.

....

....

....

When you make an evaluative response, you make a judgment about what you have read.

Connecting to Your Life

Another way to evaluate a selection is to consider how it applies to your own life. Ask yourself, "What does this story mean to me?" and "Which characters can I relate to?" and "Does the action in the story remind me of my own experiences?" When you connect a selection to your own life, the selection often becomes more meaningful to you.

"The Elevator" (continued) by William Sleator

Response notes

He was apprehensive as he approached the building after school. In the lobby, he considered the stairs. But that was ridiculous. Why should he be afraid of an old lady? If he *was* afraid of her, if he let it control him, then he was worse than all the names they called him at school. He pressed the button; he stepped into the empty elevator. He stared at the lights, urging the elevator on. It stopped on three.

At least it's not fourteen, he told himself; the person she was visiting lives on fourteen. He watched the door slide open—revealing a green coat, a piggish face, blue eyes already fixed on him as though she knew he'd be there.

It wasn't possible. It was like a nightmare. But there she was, massively real. "Going up!" he said, his voice a humiliating squeak.

She nodded, her flesh quivering, and stepped on. The door slammed. He watched her pudgy hand move toward the buttons. She pressed, not fourteen, but eighteen, the top floor, one floor above his own. The elevator trembled and began its ascent. The fat lady watched him.

He knew she had gotten on at fourteen this morning. So why was she on three, going up to eighteen now? The only floors *he* ever went to were seventeen and one. What was she doing? Had she been waiting for him? Was she riding with him on purpose?

But that was crazy. Maybe she had a lot of friends in the building. Or else she was a cleaning lady who worked in different apartments. That had to be it. He felt her eyes on him as he stared at the numbers slowly blinking on and off—slower than usual, it seemed to him. Maybe the elevator was having trouble because of how heavy she was. It was supposed to carry three adults, but it was old. What if it got stuck between floors? What if it fell?

They were on five now. It occurred to him to press seven, get off there, and walk the rest of the way. And he would have done it, if he could have reached the buttons. But there was no room to get past her without squeezing against her, and he could not bear the thought of any physical contact with her. He

129

concentrated on being in his room. He would be home soon, only another minute or so. He could stand anything for a minute, even this crazy lady watching him.

Unless the elevator got stuck between floors. Then what would he do? He tried to push the thought away, but it kept coming back. He looked at her. She was still staring at him, no expression at all on her squashed little features.

When the elevator stopped on his floor, she barely moved out of the way. He had to inch past her, rubbing against her horrible scratchy coat, terrified the door would close before he made it through. She quickly turned and watched him as the door slammed shut. And he thought, *Now she knows I live on seventeen.*

"Did you ever notice a strange fat lady on the elevator?" he asked his father that evening.

"Can't say as I have," he said, not looking away from the television.

He knew he was probably making a mistake, but he had to tell somebody. "Well, she was on the elevator with me twice today. And the funny thing was, she just kept staring at me, she never stopped looking at me for a minute. You think . . . you know of anybody who has a weird cleaning lady or anything?"

"What are you so worked up about now?" his father said, turning impatiently away from the television.

"I'm not worked up. It was just funny the way she kept staring at me. You know how people never look at each other in the elevator. Well, she just kept looking at me."

"What am I going to do with you, Martin?" his father said. He sighed and shook his head. "Honestly, now you're afraid of some poor old lady."

"I'm not afraid."

"You're afraid," said his father, with total assurance. "When are you going to grow up and act like a man? Are you going to be timid all your life?"

He managed not to cry until he got to his room—but his father probably knew he was crying anyway. He slept very little.

And in the morning, when the elevator door opened, the fat lady was waiting for him.

She was expecting him. She knew he lived on seventeen. He stood there, unable to move, and then backed away. And as he did so, her expression changed. She smiled as the door slammed.

He ran for the stairs. Luckily, the unlit flight on which he fell was between sixteen and fifteen. He only had to drag himself up one and a half flights with the terrible pain in his leg. His father was silent on the way to the hospital,

"The Elevator" (continued) by William Sleator

disappointed and annoyed at him for being such a coward and a fool.

It was a simple fracture. He didn't need a wheelchair, only a cast and crutches. But he was condemned to the elevator now. Was that why the fat lady had smiled? Had she known it would happen this way?

At least his father was with him on the elevator on the way back from the hospital. There was no room for the fat lady to get on. And even if she did, his father would see her, he would realize how peculiar she was, and then maybe he would understand. And once they got home, he could stay in the apartment for a few days—the doctor had said he should use the leg as little as possible. A week, maybe—a whole week without going on the elevator. Riding up with his father, leaning on his crutches, he looked around the little cubicle and felt a kind of triumph. He had beaten the elevator, and the fat lady, for the time being. And the end of the week was very far away.

"Oh, I almost forgot," his father reached out his hand and pressed nine.

"What are you doing? You're not getting off, are you?" he asked him, trying not to sound panicky.

"I promised Terry Ullman I'd drop in on her," his father said, looking at his watch as he stepped off.

"Let me go with you. I want to visit her, too," Martin pleaded, struggling forward on his crutches.

But the door was already closing. "Afraid to be on the elevator alone?" his father said, with a look of total scorn. "Grow up, Martin." The door slammed shut.

Martin hobbled to the buttons and pressed nine, but it didn't do any good. The elevator stopped at ten, where the fat lady was waiting for him. She moved in quickly; he was too slow, too unsteady on his crutches to work his way past her in time. The door sealed them in; the elevator started up.

"Hello, Martin," she said, and laughed, and pushed the Stop button.

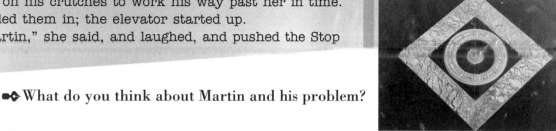

What do you think about Martin and his problem?

131

●◆Write about one connection you have with "The Elevator." You might describe what the story means to you, why you relate to one of the characters, or how the events of the story remind you of an experience you've had.

When you connect a story to your own life, the story usually becomes more meaningful to you as a reader.

Active Reading: Social Studies

Voyage with Leif Eriksson to a strange new land. Steal through darkness and danger with Harriet Tubman. March with Bella Abzug. Orbit the earth with John Glenn. Social studies can be a gateway to adventure—and active reading is the key that unlocks the gates. As with other kinds of reading, getting involved with your social studies materials can help you get the most out of them.

When you read social studies materials, several techniques can help you get involved, including:

- highlighting
- summarizing
- note-taking
- using graphics and graphic organizers

Social studies materials are full of fascinating facts. To find and remember them, try **highlighting** (marking the information that is most important as you read). Read with a marker in your hand. Scan each paragraph for the following:

- dates
- statistics
- names
- key ideas

Mark them with the highlighter to make them stand out. That way, when you review the page, they will stand out in your memory as well. (With materials that shouldn't be marked permanently, such as textbooks, take notes, as shown on pages 138–140.)

The selection below explains how Americans lived in 1940. As you read, highlight facts that you find interesting or significant.

←Response notes

134

from *The 1940s: Decade of Triumph and Trouble*
by Cabell Phillips

A young, middle-class family with a college background which had not been set back too roughly by the Depression might, with luck, count on an income in the range of $200 to $300 a month. Rent, food, and other necessities would take about two-thirds of this and the balance could be stretched to afford, perhaps, the upkeep of an automobile (most probably bought second-hand), a weekly trip to the movies, two weeks at the beach in the summer, and a modest assortment of other amenities and luxuries. A haircut cost 50¢, a glass of beer was a dime, and most doctors charged a flat fee of $2 for office visits. A good winter suit would cost the husband about $40, shirts could be had for $2, and his wife could buy a dressy wool coat for under $50. Twelve to 15 dollars would just about fill up the weekly market basket for a family of four, with milk at 13¢ a quart, eggs 35¢ a dozen, bread 8¢ a loaf, butter 35¢ a pound, pork chops 33¢ a pound, and chuck roast at 29¢. Three dollars plus a quarter tip would provide dinner for two at many good restaurants.

There were, in those Spartan days, no frozen "TV dinners" to be slipped in the oven (nor any TVs, either), no prepackaged fruit juices, no garbage grinder under the kitchen sink, no laundromat in the apartment basement, and no home air conditioning beyond what could be achieved with a couple of electric fans. Even so, a family so situated was living fairly high on the hog in terms of the national average in 1940.

❧ Would you like to have lived in 1940? Support your answer with facts from the selection.

_____

_____

_____

_____

_____

❧ Fill in the weekly budget below, using facts from the selection. (You may also need to use some basic math.) Your highlighting can help you find the facts you need. Some examples are done for you.

Weekly Budget 1940

Income (approximate): $

Expenses:

haircut

doctor appointment $ 2.00

groceries:

    1 gal. milk   .52

    1 doz. eggs

    2 loaves bread

    1 pound butter

    1 pound pork chops

    2 pounds chuck roast   .58

dinner out (for two)

new shirt

       Total expenses: $

The United States plunged into World War II in December 1941, and many raw materials and manufactured goods were suddenly needed to supply the military. By 1942, daily life in the U.S. had changed. Read the following excerpt from *The 1940s: Decade of Triumph and Trouble*, and highlight facts that show how life after the war started differed from life in 1940.

Response notes

from *The 1940s: Decade of Triumph and Trouble*
by Cabell Phillips

After 1942, a new automobile or refrigerator or radio simply was not to be had. Furniture, appliances, clothing, and scores of other necessities, all under prescribed "ceiling prices," were scarce and often shoddy. You stood in long lines to get your books of red and blue ration stamps, without which you could not buy tires and gasoline, or fuel for heating, or leather shoes, or meats, sugar, and many kinds of processed foods—and then stood in other lines hoping the supply of whatever it was you wanted would not run out before your turn came. Meanwhile, from billboard and radio you were constantly exhorted to put the money you couldn't—or shouldn't—spend into war bonds, to "Pay Your Taxes, Beat the Axis," to consider as you set out on a journey, "Is This Trip Necessary?" All in all, it was regimentation on a scale the nation had never experienced before . . . .

136

Write a paragraph comparing life in 1940 to life after 1942. Use the facts that you highlighted in both excerpts to help you decide what information to include.

....

....

....

....

....

....

....

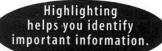
Highlighting helps you identify important information.

Two Summing Up

To make sense of social studies materials, you need to sort the main ideas from the details. One way to do this is to summarize what you read. To **summarize** is to condense: to state the **main idea** of a selection in a sentence or two. For a longer selection, a summary can also include the major points supporting the main idea.

●◆ Reread the selection by Cabell Phillips on page 134. How would you express, in one sentence, the main idea of the selection?

●◆ Imagine that you're a social studies teacher. You want to be sure that your students have grasped the basic ideas in the two selections by Cabell Phillips. Design a three-question quiz, calling for short answers (one or two sentences each). Then write the answer to each question. Your questions should reflect the main idea and major points of the selections.

137

SOCIAL STUDIES QUIZ

1.

2.

3.

Summarizing what you read helps you understand and remember it.

Three
Pulling It Together

Taking notes helps you keep track of facts and organize ideas. When you take notes, combine the skills of summarizing and scanning for details. Read the selection once to get the overall picture. Then read it a second time, and take notes. Your notes should do the following things:

- sum up the main idea of each paragraph or section
- record important names, dates, statistics, and other facts (such as causes, effects, processes, and comparisons)

World War II did not end until 1945, when the United States dropped two atomic bombs on Japan. Journalist John Hersey interviewed survivors to learn about the effects of the first bombing, which destroyed the city of Hiroshima. The following excerpt follows one survivor—the Reverend Mr. Tanimoto—as he rises early on the morning of August 6, 1945. He and his friend are using a handcart to move some church items to a safer location. As you read, take notes about Mr. Tanimoto's experiences.

from *Hiroshima* by John Hersey

Response notes →

A few minutes after they started, the air raid siren went off—a minute-long blast that warned of approaching planes but indicated to the people of Hiroshima only a slight degree of danger, since it sounded every morning at this time, when an American weather plane came over. The two men pulled and pushed the handcart through the city streets. Hiroshima was a fan-shaped city, lying mostly on the six islands formed by the seven estuarial rivers that branch out from the Ota River; its main commercial and residential districts, covering about four square miles in the center of the city, contained three-quarters of its population, which had been reduced by several evacuation programs from a wartime peak of 380,000 to about 245,000. Factories and other residential districts, or suburbs, lay compactly around the edges of the city. To the south were the docks, an airport, and the island-studded Inland Sea. A rim of mountains runs around the other three sides of the delta. Mr. Tanimoto and Mr. Matsuo took their way through the shopping center, already full of people, and across two of the rivers to the sloping streets of Koi, and up them to the outskirts and foothills. As they started up a valley away from the tight-ranked houses, the all-clear sounded. (The Japanese radar operators, detecting only three planes, supposed that they comprised a reconnaissance.) Pushing the handcart up to the rayon man's house was tiring, and the men, after they had maneuvered their load into the driveway and to the front steps, paused to rest awhile. They stood with a wing of the house between them and the city. Like most homes in this part of Japan, the house consisted of a wooden frame and wooden walls supporting a heavy tile roof. Its front hall, packed with rolls of bedding and clothing, looked like a cool cave full of fat cushions. Opposite the house, to the right of the front door, there was a large, finicky rock garden. There was no sound of planes. The morning was still; the place was cool and pleasant.

Then a tremendous flash of light cut across the sky. Mr. Tanimoto had a distinct recollection that it traveled from east to west, from the city toward the hills. It seemed a sheet of sun. Both he and Mr. Matsuo reacted in terror—and both had time to react (for they were 3,500 yards, or two miles, from the center of the explosion). Mr. Matsuo dashed up the front steps into the house and dived among the bedrolls and buried himself there. Mr. Tanimoto took four or five steps and threw himself between two big rocks in the garden. He bellied up very hard against one of them. As his face was against the stone, he did not see what happened. He felt a sudden pressure, and then splinters and pieces of board and fragments of tile fell on him. He heard no roar. (Almost no one in Hiroshima recalls hearing any noise of the bomb. But a fisherman in his sampan on the Inland Sea near Tsuzu, the man with whom Mr. Tanimoto's mother-in-law and sister-in-law were living, saw the flash and heard a tremendous explosion; he was nearly twenty miles from Hiroshima, but the thunder was greater than when the B-29s hit Iwakuni, only five miles away.)

When he dared, Mr. Tanimoto raised his head and saw that the rayon man's house had collapsed. He thought a bomb had fallen directly on it. Such clouds of dust had risen that there was a sort of twilight around. In panic, not thinking for the moment of Mr. Matsuo under the ruins, he dashed out into the street. He noticed as he ran that the concrete wall of the estate had fallen over—toward the house rather than away from it. In the street, the first thing he saw was a squad of soldiers who had been burrowing into the hillside opposite, making one of the thousands of dugouts in which the Japanese apparently intended to resist invasion, hill by hill, life for life; the soldiers were coming out of the hole, where they should have been safe, and blood was running from their heads, chests, and backs. They were silent and dazed.

Under what seemed to be a local dust cloud, the sky grew darker and darker.

● What might be some of the reasons for Mr. Tanimoto's surviving?

....

....

....

●◆Hersey gives a chronological account of Mr. Tanimoto's experiences. Based on the material in your notes, fill in the graphic below with information from Hersey's account. In the oval, write the main idea of the selection. In the rectangles, list the events that illustrate the main idea. Put them in chronological order, adding more rectangles as necessary.

Main Idea

Event 1

Event 2

Event 3

Event 4

As you read social studies materials, take notes to organize ideas and use visual organizers to clarify your thoughts.

Four

Reading the Visuals

When you read social studies materials, pay attention to more than words. Look carefully at graphics, such as charts, maps, tables, and graphs. These can give you, at a glance, as much information as several pages of writing. To get the most out of a graphic, use the following tips:

- **Read the title.** It tells you what the graphic is about.

- **Find the key.** It helps you interpret the graphic. The bar graph on the next page has the following key: ■ **Military losses** ■ **Civilian losses** The key tells you that black bars represent the number of military personnel lost in the war, and gold bars represent the number of civilians lost.

- **Read the labels.** They explain parts of the graph. In the bar graph on the next page, labels along the bottom tell you which countries the bars represent. Labels (numerals) along the side tell you the number of losses.

As you read the following excerpt from a social studies textbook, compare the information in the text to the information in the bar graph.

"Costs of World War II" from *World History*

Response notes

World War II was the most bloody and destructive war in human history. By 1945 approximately 50 million people, including soldiers and civilians, had died. Millions of others were left homeless. The greatest loss of life occurred in the Soviet Union, where approximately 20 million people perished. In addition to the human costs of the war, large areas of Europe and Asia were left in ruins. Aerial bombardment had proven particularly destructive. During the Blitz the Germans had destroyed the ancient British cathedral town of Coventry, and much of the centuries-old architecture of London. The Allies also bombed cities, subjecting Hamburg and Tokyo to terrible fire-bombings. One particularly tragic case occurred in early 1945, when Allied air forces destroyed Dresden, a German city renowned for its splendid architecture.

The destructiveness and terror of aerial bombardment reached a new peak with the atomic bomb. Although the blast at Hiroshima actually killed fewer people than conventional air raids on other Japanese and German cities, the psychological impact of a single bomb doing such enormous damage was much greater.

Perhaps the most tragic aspect of the war, however, was the scope it gave to totalitarian dictatorships to wipe out huge numbers of civilians whom they regarded as a threat to their own power. Before the war few people in the West would have believed that a country such as Germany could be the scene of a brutal crime like the Holocaust. After World War II, many people became determined to prevent such horror from ever happening again. World War II was the most destructive war in human history, costing approximately 50 million lives and leaving millions of people homeless.

Losses of the Major Wartime Powers in World War II, 1939–1945

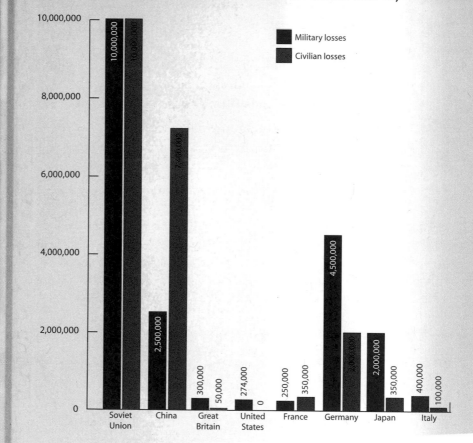

142

•◆ What information does the bar graph give you that the text does not?

....

....

....

....

....

●◆ Create a different kind of graphic that could express some or all of the information contained in the bar graph. Give your graphic a title, a key, and labels.

Graphics are compact sources of facts and statistics. When you come across a graphic in your reading, take time to examine it.

Writers of social studies textbooks use a few basic patterns to organize information. If you recognize these patterns, you can understand the information more easily. Three common patterns are:

1. **Chronological Order** The writer uses time order to tell about historical events. You used a graphic to show chronological order in the activity on page 140.

2. **Main Idea → Supporting Details** The author states a main idea and goes on to explain it with specific facts and details. The writer may close by restating the main idea, perhaps in slightly different words. Writers may use this pattern to explain reasons and results. The graphic below shows this pattern.

Topic

Main idea

Supporting detail

Supporting detail

Supporting detail

Supporting detail

3. **Comparison and Contrast** The writer shows how two things are alike and different. Authors may use this pattern to describe anything from individual people or places to entire cultures. A Venn diagram, like the one below, shows comparison and contrast.

First Thing

both

Second Thing

As you read the textbook excerpt below, pay
attention to how the writer organizes the information.

"The Atomic Bomb" from *World History*

On July 16, 1945, the first atomic bomb was successfully
tested in the desert near Alamogordo, New Mexico. Its power,
which could destroy an entire city, came from the splitting of
uranium atoms. Shortly afterward, with the support of the
British and the apparent approval of the Soviets, President
Harry Truman—who had taken office after Roosevelt's death
earlier in the year—ordered the use of atomic bombs against
Japan. He hoped to force Japan's immediate surrender.

On August 6, 1945, a lone B-29 bomber called the *Enola
Gay* flew toward Hiroshima, an important industrial and
military center in southwestern Japan. Reaching the target,
the *Enola Gay* released the single atomic weapon it carried.
The bomb detonated 2,000 feet above the city, flattening 42
square miles and killing at least 80,000 people outright.
Thousands of others soon died from the radiation released by
the bomb.

Japanese authorities, however, did not agree to surrender
immediately after the bombing of Hiroshima. Consequently, on
August 9, another atomic bomb was dropped on the city of
Nagasaki. The same day, the Soviet Union finally declared war
on Japan and promptly invaded Manchuria.

The next day Japan's emperor Hirohito decreed that his
country must surrender. In late August an Allied fleet
anchored in Tokyo Bay. There, aboard the U.S. battleship
Missouri, the Allies received Japan's formal unconditional
surrender on September 2, 1945. World War II had ended.

The selection uses chronological order to organize information. List at
least one key phrase showing chronological order in paragraphs 2, 3, and 4
of "The Atomic Bomb."

Paragraph 2:

Paragraph 3:

Paragraph 4:

◗◆Write a paragraph summarizing the selection in your own words. Instead of chronological order, try using the main idea → supporting details pattern. Begin by filling in the graphic organizer below.

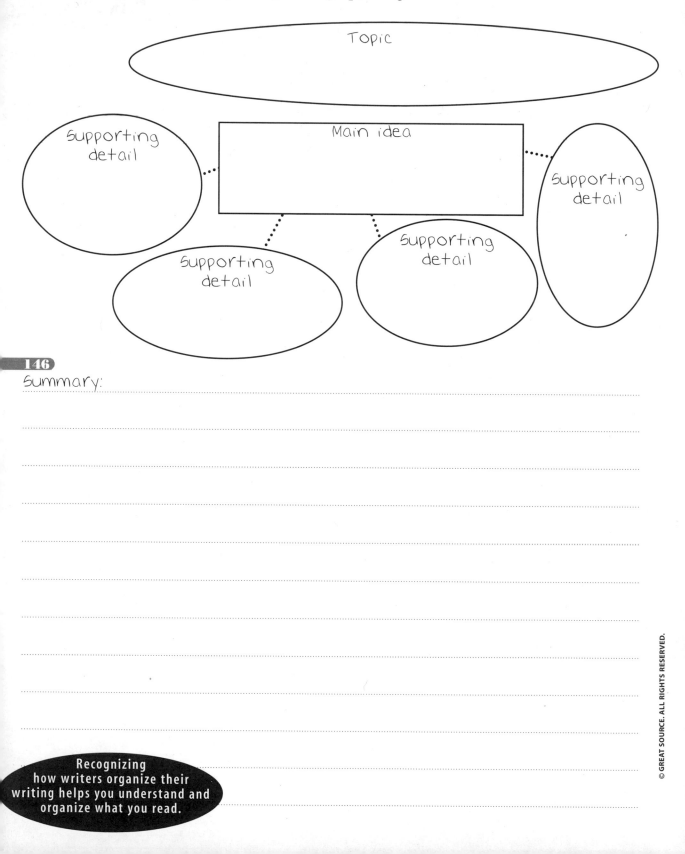

Topic

Supporting detail

Main idea

Supporting detail

Supporting detail

Supporting detail

Summary:

....

....

....

....

....

....

....

....

....

Recognizing how writers organize their writing helps you understand and organize what you read.

Active Reading: Narrative Nonfiction

What do you get when you cross fiction with nonfiction? What do you get when you cross facts with feelings?

What's the answer to these two riddles? **Narrative nonfiction**.

Narrative nonfiction is a bit of a puzzle or riddle because it is best described by what it is not. It is not fiction, although it reads like a story. It is not statistics or graphs, although it is information.

Narrative nonfiction includes biographies, autobiographies, and eyewitness accounts. Like expository nonfiction, narrative nonfiction presents information about a person, place, or thing, but it does so in the form of a story that has a beginning, a middle, and an end.

One Story *and* Facts

Narrative nonfiction is a set of **facts** (things that are known to be true) that are presented in a **story** format. The best narrative nonfiction writers know how to keep a careful balance between the information they want to present and the story elements that make that information interesting. (Story elements commonly used in narrative nonfiction include **setting, character, point of view,** and **plot.**)

As you read "The Promise," look for ways the authors balance information with narrative form. Underline any story elements that you find.

Response notes

"The Promise" from *Good Guys of Baseball*
by Terry Egan, Stan Friedmann, and Mike Levine

"Hey, Mo, there's a call for you from Boston."

Mo Vaughn can barely hear above the clear clatter of cleats and clubhouse chatter. Deep into his rap music, the Red Sox slugger is putting on his road uniform, focusing on the game ahead.

"Whoever it is, tell 'em I'll get back to them after the game," he says.

"Okay, Mo, I'll tell the kid you'll call him later."

Mo Vaughn stops everything. "Wait," he says. "I'll be right there. Tell him to hold on."

Big Mo lumbers across the clubhouse toward the phone. Opposing pitchers might find this 220-pound hulk menacing, but his young fans know better. Mo loves kids.

"Yo, Jason," says Mo. "Thanks for calling. How 'ya feeling tonight?"

He knows the boy calling from a Boston hospital is real sick.

"Yeah, this California team always gives us trouble. The game's starting soon. Now, listen pal, I want you to keep your chin up. I'll see you as soon as I get back to Boston. . . . What's that, Jason? You want me to hit a home run for you tonight? Whoa, son, I can't promise. . . . Okay, I'll give it a shot. You watch me."

Mo Vaughn hangs up the phone and shakes his head. "I really blew it this time," he whispers. "What was I thinking about, promising a home run? I'm lucky if I get a hit in this ballpark."

Mo's right. Promising a home run against ninety mile-per-hour fastballs is risky business. He's bound to disappoint Jason.

The thing is, Mo Vaughn would do anything for his young fans. Ever since he was a struggling rookie and the crusty

"The Promise" from *Good Guys of Baseball*
by Terry Egan, Stan Friedmann, and Mike Levine

Response notes

Boston fans booed him all the way back to the minors, the kids always cheered him. They helped him to hang in there. Even after he became a big-league All-Star, Mo never forgot the kids. He was always visiting schools in tough neighborhoods, pumping up the students to keep trying.

When Mo talked, they listened. He spoke the language of hope. When he hung out with sick kids at hospitals, he always made them feel better. That's where he met Jason. They became close. And on this night in California, Big Mo is trying to come through in a big way for his young buddy.

"Now batting for the Red Sox, number forty-two, Mo Vaughn."

The slugger grips his bat and marches to the plate.

"Come on, pitcher," he thinks to himself. "Give me something to hit. I can take you deep."

Mo swings hard but goes out softly. No home run.

A couple of innings later, Mo digs in again. He grips the bat even tighter.

"Come on, man, do it for the kid, you promised. He's real sick and he's counting on you."

No luck. No home run.

Mo comes up for a third chance. By now, he's kicking himself. "Never should have promised. That was stupid."

"Time!" says the ump.

Mo steps out of the batter's box and takes a breath. "Hey," thinks Mo, "you always tell Jason to keep trying. How can you give up? Get back in there and let it rip."

And when the next pitch zooms in, the big man waves his bat like a magic wand. He connects. In a heartbeat, he sends the fireball flying toward the heavens.

Higher and higher it sails.

Mo closes his eyes, puts his head down, and floats silently around the bases.

Back in Boston, a boy in a hospital has just received his friend's special delivery message. Written in the language of hope, it says, "Keep trying."

149

●◆ Try reducing "The Promise" to its most basic facts. On the trading card below, list the information that the authors give about Mo Vaughn.

Name Mo Vaughn

Number

Team

Weight

Info about player as a rookie:

Interests:

●◆ Use the facts from your trading card to write a four- or five-line bio of Mo Vaughn to be included in an "About Our Team" program book. Be sure to include all the facts that his fans might want to know.

ABOUT OUR TEAM

When you read a piece of narrative nonfiction, watch carefully for the facts the author presents.

Two

What's the Big Idea?

One of the first things to consider when reading a piece of **narrative nonfiction** is the main idea. The **main idea** is the "big idea" of a piece of writing. It is the central focus of the selection. Narrative nonfiction writers usually avoid stating the main idea directly. Instead, most writers expect readers to make **inferences** (reasonable guesses) about the main idea.

As you read this essay by Christopher de Vinck, watch carefully for the main idea. Annotate the essay by making notes in the margins and underlining phrases and sentences that you think are interesting or important.

"Power of the Powerless: A Brother's Lesson"
by Christopher de Vinck

Response notes

I grew up in the house where my brother was on his back in his bed for almost 33 years, in the same corner of his room, under the same window, beside the same yellow walls. Oliver was blind, mute. His legs were twisted. He didn't have the strength to lift his head nor the intelligence to learn anything.

Today I am an English teacher, and each time I introduce my class to the play about Helen Keller, "The Miracle Worker," I tell my students about Oliver. One day, during my first year teaching, a boy in the last row raised his hand and said, "Oh, Mr. de Vinck. You mean he was a vegetable."

I stammered for a few seconds. My family and I fed Oliver. We changed his diapers, hung his clothes and bed linen on the basement line in winter, and spread them out white and clean on the lawn in the summer. I always liked to watch the grasshoppers jump on the pillowcases.

We bathed Oliver. Tickled his chest to make him laugh. Sometimes we left the radio on in his room. We pulled the shade down over his bed in the morning to keep the sun from burning his tender skin. We listened to him laugh as we watched television downstairs. We listened to him rock his arms up and down to make the bed squeak. We listened to him cough in the middle of the night.

"Well, I guess you could call him a vegetable. I called him Oliver, my brother. You would have liked him."

One October day in 1946, when my mother was pregnant with Oliver, her second son, she was overcome by fumes from a leaking coal-burning stove. My oldest brother was sleeping in his crib, which was quite high off the ground so the gas didn't affect him. My father pulled them outside, where my mother revived quickly.

"Power of the Powerless: A Brother's Lesson"
by Christopher de Vinck

On April 20, 1947, Oliver was born. A healthy looking, plump, beautiful boy.

One afternoon, a few months later, my mother brought Oliver to a window. She held him there in the sun, the bright good sun, and there Oliver looked and looked directly into the sunlight, which was the first moment my mother realized that Oliver was blind. My parents, the true heroes of this story, learned, with the passing months, that blindness was only part of the problem. So they brought Oliver to Mt. Sinai Hospital in New York for tests to determine the extent of his condition.

The doctor said that he wanted to make it very clear to both my mother and father that there was absolutely nothing that could be done for Oliver. He didn't want my parents to grasp at false hope. "You could place him in an institution," he said. "But," my parents replied, "he is our son. We will take Oliver home of course." The good doctor answered, "Then take him home and love him."

Oliver grew to the size of a 10-year-old. He had a big chest, a large head. His hands and feet were those of a five-year-old, small and soft. We'd wrap a box of baby cereal for him at Christmas and place it under the tree; pat his head with a damp cloth in the middle of a July heat wave. His baptismal certificate hung on the wall above his head. A bishop came to the house and confirmed him.

Even now, five years after his death from pneumonia on March 12, 1980, Oliver still remains the weakest, most helpless human being I ever met, and yet he was one of the most powerful human beings I ever met. He could do absolutely nothing except breathe, sleep, eat, and yet he was responsible for action, love, courage, insight. When I was small my mother would say, "Isn't it wonderful that you can see?" And once she said, "When you go to heaven, Oliver will run to you, embrace you, and the first thing he will say is 'Thank you.'" I remember, too, my mother explaining to me that we were blessed with Oliver in ways that were not clear to her at first.

So often parents are faced with a child who is severely retarded, but who is also hyperactive, demanding or wild, who needs constant care. So many people have little choice but to place their child in an institution. We were fortunate that Oliver didn't need us to be in his room all day. He never knew what his condition was. We were blessed with his presence, a true presence of peace.

When I was in my early 20s I met a girl and fell in love. After a few months I brought her home to meet my family. When my mother went to the kitchen to prepare dinner, I

"Power of the Powerless: A Brother's Lesson"
by Christopher de Vinck

Response notes

asked the girl, "Would you like to see Oliver?" for I had told her about my brother. "No," she answered.

Soon after, I met Roe, a lovely girl. She asked me the names of my brothers and sisters. She loved children. I thought she was wonderful. I brought her home after a few months to meet my family. Soon it was time for me to feed Oliver. I remember sheepishly asking Roe if she'd like to see him. "Sure," she said.

I sat at Oliver's bedside as Roe watched over my shoulder. I gave him his first spoonful, his second. "Can I do that?" Roe asked with ease, with freedom, with compassion, so I gave her the bowl and she fed Oliver one spoonful at a time.

The power of the powerless. Which girl would you marry? Today Roe and I have three children.

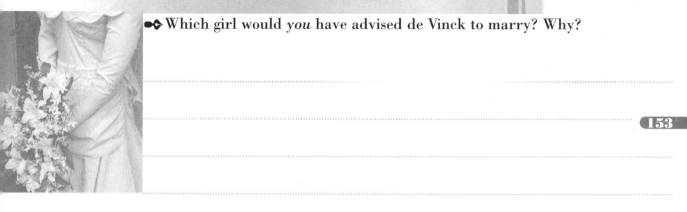

●◆ Which girl would *you* have advised de Vinck to marry? Why?

153

●❖ What is de Vinck's main idea in "Power of the Powerless"? Explain it here.

●❖ Now begin planning your own narrative nonfiction account. Brainstorm a list of possible essay topics. (Use the space below to make some notes.) When you've finished, write your main idea.

154

In narrative nonfiction, the main idea is usually implied. Once you find the main idea, you can begin to consider the message the author has for you.

My main idea:

Three

Details, Details

Readers can be demanding. They expect interesting stories, good narration, and lots of action. They also expect plenty of details. The most skillful nonfiction writers know that a high level of detail is just as important to nonfiction as it is to fiction.

In narrative nonfiction, **details** are the words, phrases, and sentences the author uses to:

• support the main idea
• act as a "hook" that motivates readers to stay involved
• help readers visualize what the author describes

➥ Reread "Power of the Powerless." Circle any details that are interesting or important. Then use the graphic below to show the relationship between de Vinck's main idea and his most important details. Be sure to explain how each detail relates to the main idea.

de Vinck's main idea

155

| detail | detail | detail | detail |

➥ Reflect on the main idea you wrote for Lesson Two. What details could you use to support this idea? List some here.

•

•

•

Details are important because they help the reader visualize a scene and get involved in the writing.

FOUR Inferencing

Whenever you read, you make **inferences** (reasonable guesses) about the author's underlying message. This is true for both fiction and nonfiction. When you read narrative nonfiction, many of the inferences you make will be about the "character" of the piece. In a **biography,** you'll make inferences about the person described. (For example, think about the selection you read for Lesson One. What inferences can you make about Mo Vaughn?) In an **autobiography,** you make inferences about the person who does the describing.

As you read this selection, watch for information about the narrator. Underline any clues you find about her personality.

Response notes

This is important to her

concentration camp survivor

from ***I Have Lived a Thousand Years*** by Livia Bitton-Jackson

On April 30, 1995, I took an El-Al flight from Tel Aviv to Munich. From the terminal I took the S-Bahn to Tutzing, and from there I was driven to Seeshaupt, a small Bavarian resort. This was not an easy journey to take, and I took it after some weeks of deliberation. I was going back to Germany—fifty years later.

It was in Seeshaupt on this very day fifty years ago that the American army had liberated me, along with my brother and my mother and thousands of other skeletal prisoners. Some leading citizens of Seeshaupt had decided to commemorate the event. They formed a committee and dispatched letters of invitation to possible survivors all over the world. One such letter reached me in my New York home, and here I was, making a detour, on a Tel Aviv–New York flight, to Seeshaupt.

The former mayor's son, then a nine-year-old boy, remembered how the victorious Allies had led his father and his family and all other members of the local elite to the Seeshaupt train station, where they witnessed a most horrifying picture of human suffering. The sight of thousands of disfigured corpses and maimed, dying skeletons left an indelible mark on his awareness.

Now he is a doctor in Seeshaupt, and when his patients, members of the post-war generation, refused to believe his account of what he saw, he decided to bring back survivors of that ghastly liberation as living proof that the unbelievable did happen.

The sky was overcast and a light drizzle veiled my view as my host, Dr. Peter Westebbe, one of the local organizers of the commemoration, drove me through the streets of Seeshaupt to the dedication ceremony.

Eighteen survivors had arrived for the ceremony from all over the world. Some were from the United States, some from

from *I Have Lived a Thousand Years* by Livia Bitton-Jackson

Response notes

South America, some from Israel, and one from Greece. The townspeople were there—about three hundred, mostly young. The present mayor of the town officiated at the dedication of a monument to those who had died and those who had survived to be liberated here—over two thousand five hundred, according to records. Young children from the local school planted trees, danced and sang, and the pastor of the local church blessed the monument. The local audience was visibly moved.

We, the eighteen survivors who had returned to Seeshaupt, men and women in their sixties and seventies, briefly reminisced about that liberation day fifty years ago, and as we looked into each other's eyes, we saw that the years had not faded the pain of memories. The pain was intact. And so was the sense of overwhelming burden.

A celebration followed the dedication ceremony. Several hundred guests filled the local beer hall, where tables were set up for a festive meal and musical entertainment by the local band.

Quietly I slipped out of the hall, and slowly made my way to the train station. Late Sunday afternoon stillness enveloped the small town. I walked along the tracks to the colorless, deserted, memorable platform. No trains. No passengers anywhere. Total emptiness. Only an incessant, light drizzle.

But for me the platform was full. It was brimming with a disarray of sights, hundreds upon hundreds, a bleeding carpet of dead and dying. I saw Greco, the fifteen-year-old Greek boy with enormous, feverish eyes, begging for water. I saw Lilli, the sixteen-year-old brunette with her leg blown off, sitting in a pool of blood. I heard Martha, blinded in both eyes, calling to her mother. And Beth, and Irene . . . ageless faces, skeletal limbs filled the gray, translucent mist.

"There are no more trains today." I turned around, startled. The woman with the unmistakably Bavarian accent had a pleasant, nondescript face. "There are no more trains today from this station."

"Thank you. I'm not waiting for a train."

She waited, wondering; then, with a hint of suspicion lingering in her manner, she reluctantly walked on.

But the moment was gone. The half-century-old visions were no longer retrievable onto the screen of my present reality. A cold, opaque haze enveloped the tracks; the platform and the grim two-story station house were empty.

I walked back to the beer hall, where the celebration was winding down. "What message do you have for us?" one of the committee members asked me. "What lessons?"

157

from *I Have Lived a Thousand Years* by Livia Bitton-Jackson

I pondered the question. I was fourteen when the war ended, and believed that the evil of the Holocaust was defeated along with the forces that brought it about. Six years later a new life began for me in the New World. A new life, free of threat. A new world, full of hope.

In America I grew from traumatized teen to grandmotherhood. And as the world grew more and more advanced technologically, it seemed to grow more and more tolerant of terror and human suffering.

My fears have returned. And yet my hope, my dream, of a world free of human cruelty and violence has not vanished.

My hope is that learning about past evils will help us to avoid them in the future. My hope is that by learning what horrors can result from prejudice and intolerance, we can cultivate a commitment to fight prejudice and intolerance.

It is for this reason that I wrote my recollections of the horror. Only one who was there can truly tell the tale. And I was there.

For you, the third generation, the Holocaust has slipped into the realm of history, or legend. Or, into the realm of sensational subjects on the silver screen. Reading my personal account I believe you will feel—you will know—that the Holocaust was neither a legend nor Hollywood fiction but a lesson for the future. A lesson to help future generations prevent the causes of the twentieth-century catastrophe from being transmitted into the twenty-first.

My stories are of gas chambers, shootings, electrified fences, torture, scorching sun, mental abuse, and constant threat of death.

But they are also stories of faith, hope, triumph, and love. They are stories of perseverance, loyalty, courage in the face of overwhelming odds, and of never giving up.

My story is my message: Never give up.

●◆ **What is your reaction to Bitton-Jackson's story?**

●◆Who is Livia Bitton-Jackson? What kind of person is she? Review the inferences you made while reading the selection. Then use the chart below to help you decide what you know and what you can infer.

What I know about Bitton-Jackson	What I've inferred about Bitton-Jackson

●◆Now use your notes and inferences to help you write a short personality profile of Livia Bitton-Jackson.

159

Making inferences about a character helps you build a portrait of the person you are reading about.

Five

The **inferences** you make while reading a piece of narrative nonfiction can also help you determine the author's purpose (or intent) for writing. **Author's purpose** is the reason(s) why an author writes. Authors write to entertain, to inform or explain, to persuade or argue, or to express personal thoughts or feelings. In most nonfiction, including narrative nonfiction, the author will make a direct statement of purpose. Look for it as you read.

Reread the excerpt from Bitton-Jackson's memoir. Underline those parts in which she discusses her purpose.

●◆ In one or two sentences, explain Bitton-Jackson's purpose.

....

....

....

....

160

●◆ In your opinion, does Bitton-Jackson succeed in achieving her purpose? Explain.

....

....

....

....

....

....

In narrative nonfiction, writers often make a direct statement of their purpose. Once you understand the author's intent, you can understand the idea or message the author has for you.

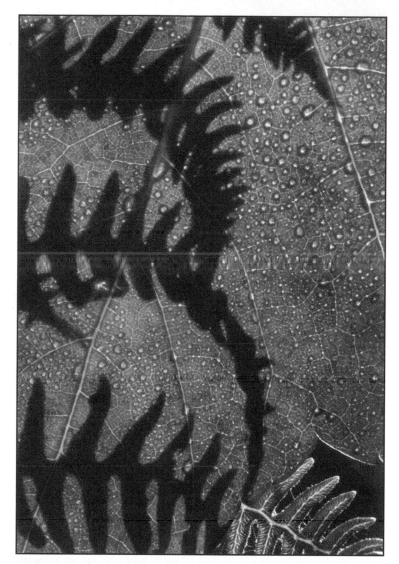

Style and Structure

Style is how an author uses words and phrases to form his or her ideas. Style is all about choice, word choices, sentence choices, choices about dialogue, description, figurative language, tone, and so on.

The structure of a piece of writing is the way it is put together. Structure is the arrangement of words into a sentence and sentences into paragraphs.

Every once in a while style and structure fight each other for dominance or control. More often they blend together so well that you can't tell one from the other. You simply end up with a perfect sentence—or a perfect piece of writing.

One

Style Choices

Style is how an author writes—his or her choice and arrangement of words. When you are asked to analyze an author's style, you might start by thinking about the author's word choices. Ask yourself questions such as:

1. Is the author's language formal or informal?

2. Is the author's vocabulary simple or complex or somewhere in between?

3. Does the author use **sensory language**—that is, words that can help you see, hear, touch, smell, or taste the thing described?

Read the following selections by John Steinbeck and Judith Ortiz Cofer. As you read, make notes about the various word choices each author makes.

Response Notes

162

from *The Pearl* by John Steinbeck

The sun was warming the brush house, breaking through its crevices in long streaks. And one of the streaks fell on the hanging box where Coyotito lay, and on the ropes that held it.

It was a tiny movement that drew their eyes to the hanging box. Kino and Juana froze in their positions. Down the rope that hung the baby's box from the roof support a scorpion moved slowly. His stinging tail was straight out behind him, but he could whip it up in a flash of time.

Kino's breath whistled in his nostrils and he opened his mouth to stop it. And then the startled look was gone from him and the rigidity from his body. In his mind a new song had come, the Song of Evil, the music of the enemy, of any foe of the family, a savage, secret, dangerous melody, and underneath, the Song of the Family cried plaintively.

The scorpion moved delicately down the rope toward the box. Under her breath Juana repeated an ancient magic to guard against such evil, and on top of that she muttered a Hail Mary between clenched teeth. But Kino was in motion. His body glided quietly across the room, noiselessly and smoothly. His hands were in front of him, palms down, and his eyes were on the scorpion. Beneath it in the hanging box Coyotito laughed and reached up his hand toward it. It sensed danger when Kino was almost within reach of it. It stopped, and its tail rose up over its back in little jerks and the curved thorn on the tail's end glistened.

Kino stood perfectly still. He could hear Juana whispering the old magic again, and he could hear the evil music of the enemy. He could not move until the scorpion moved, and it felt for the source of the death that was coming to it. Kino's hand went forward very slowly, very smoothly. The thorned tail jerked upright. And at that moment the laughing Coyotito shook the rope and the scorpion fell.

from *The Pearl* by John Steinbeck

Kino's hand leaped to catch it, but it fell past his fingers, fell on the baby's shoulder, landed and struck. Then, snarling, Kino had it, had it in his fingers, rubbing it to a paste in his hands. He threw it down and beat it into the earth floor with his fist, and Coyotito screamed with pain in his box. But Kino beat and stamped the enemy until it was only a fragment and a moist place in the dirt. His teeth were bared and fury flared in his eyes and the Song of the Enemy roared in his ears.

●◆ Answer the following questions about Steinbeck's word choices.

Is Steinbeck's language: formal?   informal?   somewhere in-between?
Example:

Is his vocabulary: simple?   complex?   somewhere in-between?
Example:

Does Steinbeck use sensory language in *The Pearl?*   yes   no
Example:

Now read this selection by Judith Ortiz Cofer.

163

from **"The Story of My Body"** by Judith Ortiz Cofer

I was born a white girl in Puerto Rico but became a brown girl when I came to live in the United States. My Puerto Rican relatives called me tall; at the American school, some of my rougher classmates called me Skinny Bones, and the Shrimp because I was the smallest member of my classes all through grammar school until high school, when the midget Gladys was given the honorary post of front row center for class pictures and scorekeeper, bench warmer, in P. E. I reached my full stature of five feet in sixth grade.

I started out life as a pretty baby and learned to be a pretty girl from a pretty mother. Then at ten years of age I suffered one of the worst cases of chicken pox I have ever heard of. My entire body, including the inside of my ears and in between my toes, was covered with pustules which in a fit of panic at my appearance I scratched off my face, leaving permanent scars. A cruel school nurse told me I would always have them—tiny cuts that looked as if a mad cat had plunged its claws deep into my skin. I grew my hair long and hid behind it for the first years of my adolescence. This was when I learned to be invisible.

Now answer the same word choice questions about Cofer's style that you answered about Steinbeck's.

Is Cofer's language: formal?   informal?   somewhere in-between?
Example:

Is her vocabulary: simple?   complex?   somewhere in-between?
Example:

Does she use sensory language in her story?   yes   no
Example:

Use the Venn diagram below to compare Steinbeck's word choices to Cofer's word choices. On the lines marked "e.g.," give examples from the writing to support what you say.

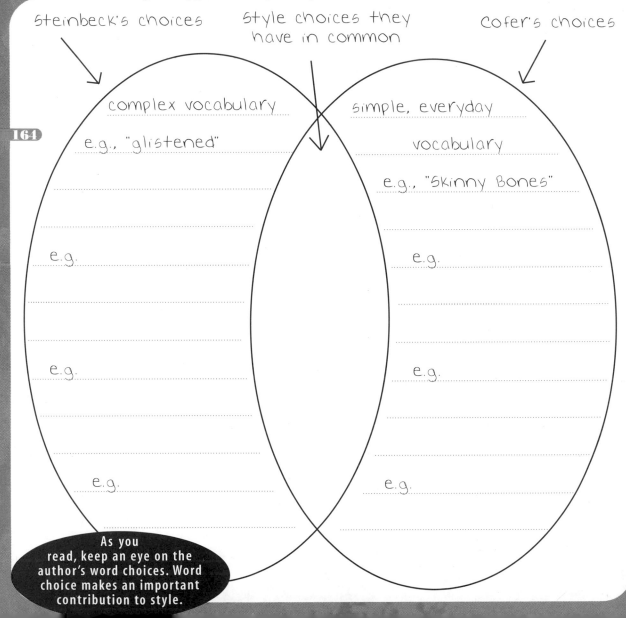

Steinbeck's choices   Style choices they   Cofer's choices
                             have in common

complex vocabulary   simple, everyday
e.g., "glistened"   vocabulary
                                             e.g., "Skinny Bones"

e.g.   e.g.

e.g.   e.g.

e.g.   e.g.

As you read, keep an eye on the author's word choices. Word choice makes an important contribution to style.

Two
More Style Choices

There are many elements, in addition to word choice, that play an important role in an author's style. **Style** involves all kinds of choices, including:

✔ sentence length

✔ amount of **dialogue**

✔ amount of **description**

✔ number of figurative expressions used (**simile** and **metaphor**, for example)

✔ **tone** (how the writer or writing "sounds"—suspenseful, scary, joyful, and so on)

➤ Think about Steinbeck's and Cofer's writing. Use the grid below to check off the style choices that apply to each author.

	Steinbeck	Cofer
long sentences		
short sentences		
a lot of dialogue		
a little dialogue		
no dialogue		
a lot of description		
a little description		
figurative expressions used		
no figurative expressions used		
suspenseful tone		
casual tone		

165

◆◆Using information from your diagram and charts, describe the differences between Steinbeck's and Cofer's styles. How does each writer's style fit the subject that he or she is writing about?

Writers make many different choices when it comes to style, including sentence length, dialogue, description, use of figurative language, and tone.

Three
The Structure

Structure means how the writing is put together. Even the shortest, simplest selections are usually structured very carefully. What comes first in the story? What comes last? How many stanzas should I use? These are some of the questions that writers ask themselves when they consider the structure of their writing.

Authors often structure their writing in a way that will help you, the reader, make a fast and strong connection with the story. This is why so many novels and short stories begin with an exciting plot twist—a murder, for example, or an explosion at the factory down the street.

As you read this selection from Joyce Hansen's novel, make some notes about its structure.

---

from ***I Thought My Soul Would Rise and Fly*** by Joyce Hansen

Monday, April 24, 1865

Response notes

Dear Friend,

I saw Yankees for the first time today when I was carrying milk from the dairy house. I tried to see why Master calls them vulgar and uncouth, but I still don't understand. They look no different from the white men I have always seen. They didn't have no horns either. Friend, I can't say whether or not they had tails. I thought it would be rude to ask.

Early this morning three of them rode up the drive leading to The House. When the soldiers reached the cottages, they stopped their horses. Master and Mistress seemed small and old, but they held their heads as high as the pine trees surrounding The House. They talked to the soldiers at length, but I do not know what was said.

While I was sweeping the passageway that separates the kitchen from The House, Master called everyone, including the field hands, to the yard. He stood between the gleaming white columns of The House as he talked to us. "The government says I have to pay you wages now. If you remain, your pay will be one tenth of the cotton crop you bring in, and you can live in your same cabins."

Then he looked at James, Cook, and Ruth and said, "I will pay you ten dollars a month and provide food as in the past." He didn't say anything to Nancy or Miriam—much less me. Maybe because we are the youngest of the house slaves.

One of the Yankee soldiers spoke next. I had to listen closely to understand his words for his speech sounded so different from ours, as if he was talking through his nose.

He explained that he is from some place called the Freedmen's Bureau and that the Bureau is helping former

Response notes

slaves adjust to being free. "You must behave yourselves and work as you are accustomed. All field hands must sign a yearly work contract. Anyone found roaming about the countryside without a job or a place to live will be arrested for vagrancy."

Everyone was silent. I counted eighty field hands, men and women, and not a one was smiling. Even the birds stopped singing. Then one of the hands named Douglass spoke. Douglass used to always do chores for Mistress at special times, like take down the drapes when it was time for cleaning The House for Christmas. He was a boy then, but now he is a thin, handsome young man and works in the fields with his mother and sister. "Sir," Douglass said. "Tell me one thing. Is we free?"

Then other people started calling out, too. The Yankee shushed them. He told us that we are free, but whoever doesn't work and follow the rules will be jailed. He says we are not free to roam about and cause trouble.

Then the man everyone calls Brother Solomon, because he does the preaching in the arbor on Sundays, spoke to the soldier. "Sir, we will not stay here 'less we get a school for our young ones and land for us to farm for our own selves."

Master turned a slow red and Mistress stared at Brother Solomon with angry gray eyes. I was surprised to see her look at him that way. She and Master always said he was the best hand they had. Brother Solomon is headman over the field hands and helps the overseer. He also makes sure the gardens and the orchards are taken care of.

Master said to Brother Solomon that if they stay, he will give each family five acres of land and a plantation school. The hands smiled and so did I. Imagine a school on Davis Hall Plantation.

But one of the elderly women, her hands shaking as she held on to her walking stick, asked what would happen to the old people who can't bring in a crop anymore. She began to cry and she made me almost cry as well.

One of the soldiers spoke before Master answered and told her that elderly people cannot be thrown off farms and plantations. Master has a responsibility to care for them.

Then Brother Solomon spoke to the woman. "Mother Naomi, we all in this cauldron together. We take care of you."

Friend, if I was a brave girl, I'd have asked that Yankee whether I would be punished if I limped on upstairs to Master's library and started reading and writing. Master never did say we was free, but I guess we are. I can't wait until we get a school. I'll be the first pupil there.

—Patsy

168

●◆Like most stories, this selection has a structure, with a beginning, a climax, and a resolution. Use the graphic below to examine how Hansen structured Patsy's story.

Beginning

Climax

Resolution

●◆What's the effect of Hansen's choice of structure on your understanding and interest in Patsy's story? How has she changed from the beginning of the story?

Patsy at the beginning	Patsy at the end

A writer can use structure to help readers connect with a story.

Four

Poetic Structure

Poets often put a lot of thought into the structure of their poems since many poets use structure to help reveal their meaning. Read this poem by E. E. Cummings. What is the first thing you notice?

Response notes

l(a
E. E. Cummings

l(a

le
af
fa

ll

s)
one
l

iness

➥ In this poem, Cummings explores the idea of loneliness, and how it feels to be alone. How does his "falling leaf" structure help reveal that meaning?

....

....

....

....

....

Now read "Saying Yes" by Diana Chang. Make notes about the poem's structure as you read.

Response notes

Saying Yes
Diana Chang

"Are you Chinese?"
"Yes."

"American?"
"Yes."

"*Really* Chinese?"
"No . . . not quite."

"*Really* American?"
"Well, actually, you see . . ."

But I would rather say
yes

Not neither-nor,
Not maybe,
but both, and not only

The homes I've had,
the ways I am

I'd rather say it
twice,
yes

●◆ Are all of Chang's stanzas structured the same? Use this chart to make notes about her structure. What can you observe about her stanzas?

Stanza	Structure
1	Two lines: one is a question; the other is only one word. Both lines are dialogue.
2	
3	
4	
5	
6	
7	
8	

●◆ What is Chang's message? Does her structure help reveal it? Explain.

When you read a poem, note its structure. Poets sometimes use structure to help reveal their meaning.

Five
Structure *and* Style

Once you understand the basics of **style** and **structure**, you can evaluate an author's use of these elements. What do I think about Cummings's style? his structure? These are the kinds of questions critical readers ask when they evaluate style and structure.

Of course, everyone has his or her own opinion about what makes for an engaging structure and style. Here's your chance to note your responses to the selections you read in this unit.

●◆First, make a list of criteria you will use to evaluate each piece in terms of style and structure. (Review the previous lessons in this unit to help you decide on your criteria.)

Criteria for style

Criteria for structure

➡◆Use your criteria to complete the chart.

Selection	What I thought about the structure	What I thought about the style
The Pearl		
"The Story of My Body"		
I Thought My Soul Would Rise and Fly		
"l(a"		
"Saying Yes"		

Before you evaluate style and structure, first decide on criteria to use for the evaluation.

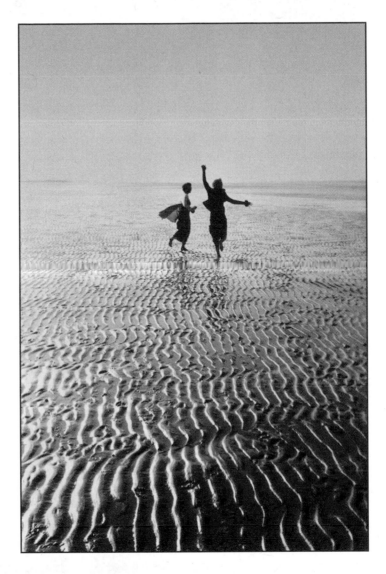

Poetic Forms and Techniques

A gentleman dining at Crewe
Found quite a large mouse in his stew.

These lines are the beginning of a limerick. A poet would probably not choose this form for a poem about a serious subject like death or loneliness, because limericks are meant to be amusing. When a poet composes, he or she has many choices to make. What form should the poem take? How will the subject of the poem be reflected in the form? Should the poem follow a set pattern of sounds? Or should the poem sound like one side of a conversation? In this unit, you will find out more about the choices that poets make and why they make them.

One
Breaking the Rules

In some ways, writing can be thought of as a game. The words are your game pieces, and, when you write a sentence that moves your readers or makes them stop and think, you "win." And like all games, the game of writing has some rules, such as ending a statement with a period or capitalizing proper nouns.

But not all writers follow the rules. For instance, a poet may choose to disobey the rules of punctuation. The poet might do this in order to reflect a particular message, evoke a specific feeling, or simply to express thoughts in an unconventional way. When you come across a poem that doesn't follow the rules, ask yourself, "Why did this poet use unusual punctuation? How would the poem be different if the punctuation were conventional?" As you read "I'm Nobody," circle any unusual punctuation.

Response notes

I'm Nobody
Emily Dickinson

I'm Nobody! Who are you?
Are you—Nobody—too?
Then there's a pair of us?
Don't tell! they'd advertise—you know!

How dreary—to be—Somebody!
How public—like a Frog—
To tell your name—the livelong June—
To an admiring Bog!

❧ How does the speaker feel about being "Nobody"? How can you tell?

176

●✦ What do you think Dickinson is saying in this poem?

●✦ Dickinson ends the first three lines of her poem with question marks. Several of the lines that follow end with exclamation points. What does the change in punctuation reveal about the speaker's feelings and how they change?

Poets sometimes choose punctuation that is unconventional to emphasize a point. When you see that happen in a poem, try to figure out why the poet wrote the poem that way.

Two

Patterns of Sound

Putting together a poem is a lot like staging a play. You could have a great story and award-winning actors, but without scenery, costumes, lighting, and special effects, the play would not be as meaningful. A poem needs "extras" like these, too. Sound patterns in a poem can support the leading players—the words and the message.

As you read a poem, look for sound patterns. You might find the **repetition** of words and phrases, a pattern of **rhyming** words, or a certain **rhythm** that repeats throughout the work. Ask yourself, "Why did the poet choose to use these sound patterns? How do the sound patterns make me feel as I read? How do the sound patterns reinforce the meaning of the poem?"

Consider these questions as you read "O Captain! My Captain!" Jot down your ideas in the response notes.

Response notes

O Captain! My Captain!
Walt Whitman

O Captain! my Captain! our fearful trip is done,
The ship has weather'd every rack, the prize we sought is won,
The port is near, the bells I hear, the people all exulting,
While follow eyes the steady keel, the vessel grim and daring;
   But O heart! heart! heart!
    O the bleeding drops of red,
     Where on the deck my Captain lies,
      Fallen cold and dead.

O Captain! my Captain! rise up and hear the bells;
Rise up—for you the flag is flung—for you the bugle trills,
For you bouquets and ribbon'd wreaths—for you the shores a-crowding
For you they call, the swaying mass, their eager faces turning;
   Here Captain! dear father!
    This arm beneath your head!
     It is some dream that on the deck,
      You've fallen cold and dead.

My captain does not answer, his lips are pale and still,
My father does not feel my arm, he has no pulse nor will,
The ship is anchor'd safe and sound, its voyage closed and done,
From fearful trip the victor ship comes in with object won:
   Exult O shores, and ring O bells!
    But I with mournful tread,
     Walk the deck my Captain lies,
      Fallen cold and dead.

178

●◆ Read the poem aloud to get the full effect of the pattern of rhyme and rhythm. How do the rhyme and rhythm of the poem make you feel as you read? Why do you think Whitman chose this rhyme and rhythm to convey the subject of the poem?

●◆ Whitman also uses the technique of repeating words and phrases. Go back to the poem and circle words and phrases that are repeated. Then note them in the chart. Write what you think Walt Whitman wanted to emphasize by using the repetition.

Repeated Word	Effects of Repeating the Word
Captain	

●◆Using the information in the poem, write a news article about the battle, the homecoming, and the fate of the captain.

Daily News

●◆Which do you think conveys a stronger message—
the poem or your news article? Explain.

Poets
use sound patterns to
emphasize certain points and
to create an overall feeling that
cannot always be created
through prose writing.

Three
The Sonnet

A triangle is a figure with three sides. A figure with four sides can only be called a *square* if all four sides are the same length. Just as there are formulas to describe geometric shapes, there are also formulas to describe certain types of poems. Some of these formulas have been used by poets for hundreds of years. One form, the limerick, uses a certain pattern of rhythm and rhyme and is almost always used for humorous and nonsense verses. **Sonnets** are another type of patterned poem.

The dialogue in this excerpt from Shakespeare's *Romeo and Juliet* is in the form of a sonnet. These are the first words exchanged by Romeo and Juliet when they meet at a masquerade ball. Romeo is dressed as a pilgrim. As you read, try to figure out the pattern of the sonnet.

From ***Romeo and Juliet*** by William Shakespeare

Response notes

ROMEO If I profane with my unworthiest hand
        This holy shrine, the gentle sin is this;
        My lips, two blushing pilgrims, ready stand
        To smooth that rough touch with a tender kiss.
JULIET Good pilgrim, you do wrong your hand too much,
        Which mannerly devotion shows in this;
        For saints have hands that pilgrims' hands do touch,
        And palm to palm is holy palmers' kiss.
ROMEO Have not saints lips, and holy palmers too?
JULIET Ay, pilgrim, lips that they must use in prayer.
ROMEO O! then, dear saint, let lips do what hands do;
        They pray, Grant thou, lest faith turn to despair.
JULIET Saints do not move, though grant for prayers' sake.
ROMEO Then move not, while my prayer's effect I take.

181

What is the gist of Romeo and Juliet's conversation?

●◆Use the excerpt from *Romeo and Juliet* to analyze the "formula" for a sonnet.

1. How many lines does the excerpt have? _____

   All sonnets have this number of lines.

2. Sonnets are divided into sets of lines. The first twelve lines are divided into three four-line sets called *quatrains*. The last two lines are called a *couplet*.

   Mark the quatrains and the couplet in the excerpt.

3. In many sonnets, each quatrain presents some examples and the couplet presents a conclusion. Does this excerpt follow this pattern? Explain why or why not.

4. Another part of the sonnet "formula" is the rhyme scheme. Circle the words in the poem that rhyme and connect the pairs of words with a line. An example is done for you.

●◆Some poets use the form of the sonnet because it is a traditional form. What other reasons do you think a poet might have for choosing to use this pattern for a poem? List three possible reasons.

A sonnet is a traditional form for a poem. When you read a sonnet, try to figure out why the poet chose that form to express his or her ideas.

Four Haiku

ave you ever read a telegram? Instead of saying, "My plane touched down safely. I am enjoying spending time in this country, and I look forward to coming home soon," a telegram says, "Plane landed. Having fun. Home soon!" A *haiku* is a type of poem that is a lot like a telegram. It captures a moment, a feeling, or something that catches the poet's eye in just a few words.

Haiku follow a set pattern, and they often have nature as their subject matter. Haiku generally have three lines, with the first and third line each having five syllables and the middle line having seven. As you read Richard Wright's "Four Haiku," think about how each **stanza** brings something into focus.

Four Haiku
Richard Wright

A balmy spring wind
Reminding me of something
I cannot recall.

The green cockleburrs
Caught in the thick wooly hair
Of the black boy's head.

Standing in the field,
I hear the whispering of
Snowflake to snowflake.

It is September
The month in which I was born,
And I have no thoughts.

Response notes

183

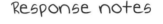

↪ Go back to the poem and circle the images of nature that Wright uses. How do these images of nature show a contrast between childhood and adulthood?

●◆ Try your hand at writing haiku. Remember that the goal of haiku is to capture a moment or a feeling in a small amount of space. Write three different haiku verses. Then circle the one that you think gives the most complete "snapshot."

●◆ What do you think are some of the advantages and disadvantages of using this poetic form to express ideas?

Advantages	Disadvantages

Poets use haiku to express ideas simply and compactly. When you are reading haiku, try to figure out what the poet wants to reveal about the subject of the poem by expressing ideas in this way.

Five Free Verse

There are almost as many kinds of poems as there are poets. Poems can be any length, have any (or no) pattern of rhyme, follow a strict form, or follow no form at all. Poems that don't follow a set form are called **free verse**. Free verse poems don't "sound" a certain way. As you read "Hannah Armstrong," note characteristics of the poem that you find especially striking.

Hannah Armstrong
Edgar Lee Masters

I wrote him a letter asking him for old times' sake
To discharge my sick boy from the army;
But maybe he couldn't read it.
Then I went to town and had James Garber,
Who wrote beautifully, write him a letter;
But maybe that was lost in the mails.
So I traveled all the way to Washington.
I was more than an hour finding the White House.
And when I found it they turned me away,
Hiding their smiles. Then I thought:
"Oh, well, he ain't the same as when I boarded him
And he and my husband worked together
And all of us called him Abe, there in Menard."
As a last attempt I turned to a guard and said:
"Please say it's old Aunt Hannah Armstrong
From Illinois, come to see him about her sick boy
In the army."
Well, just in a moment they let me in!
And when he saw me he broke in a laugh,
And dropped his business as president,
And wrote in his own hand Doug's discharge,
Talking the while of the early days,
And telling stories.

Response notes

185

What do you think of this poem?

●◆ What are some of the similarities and differences between sonnets, haiku, and free verse? Create a graphic, such as a Venn diagram or chart, to illustrate these similarities and differences.

●◆ Even though free verse has no regular rhythm or rhyme, it is a form of poetry. Why do you think this is the case? Use your graphic to help explain your answer.

Poets can use free verse to express their thoughts without using set patterns of rhyme or rhythm.

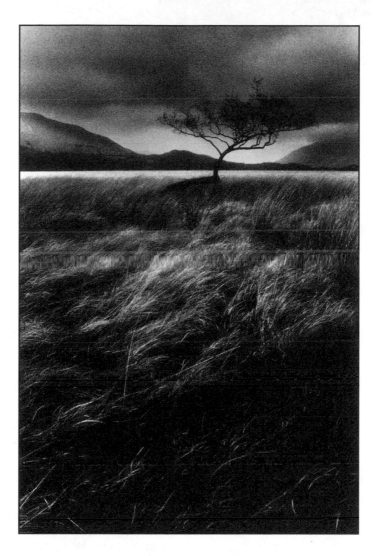

Active Reading: Persuasive Writing

Wouldn't it be great if you could win every argument and triumph in every debate? Wouldn't it be terrific if you could be sure that no matter what you say or do, you're going to convince your audience to agree with your viewpoint?

Unfortunately, there are no guarantees when it comes to debating or persuading. However, there are a few tried-and-true techniques that can help you. In this unit, you'll learn some important elements of persuasion. You'll also learn how three of history's finest persuasive speakers used these elements to help clinch their arguments.

Viewpoint is the author's perspective on an issue or topic. The author's viewpoint may be presented as a position statement: "We need more playgrounds and fewer new landfills."

In some persuasive writing, the author makes a direct statement of his or her viewpoint. Other times the author gives hints about his or her viewpoint but doesn't actually come right out and state it. Instead, the author expects the reader to make **inferences** (reasonable guesses) about the purpose of the argument. Read Abraham Lincoln's "Gettysburg Address." Underline words and phrases that give you clues about Lincoln's viewpoint.

Response notes

"Gettysburg Address" by Abraham Lincoln

Four score and seven years ago our fathers brought forth on this continent, a new nation, conceived in Liberty, and dedicated to the proposition that all men are created equal.

Now we are engaged in a great civil war, testing whether that nation, or any nation so conceived and so dedicated, can long endure. We are met on a great battlefield of that war. We have come to dedicate a portion of that field as a final resting place for those who here gave their lives that that nation might live. It is altogether fitting and proper that we should do this.

But, in a larger sense, we cannot dedicate—we cannot consecrate—we cannot hallow—this ground. The brave men, living and dead, who struggled here have consecrated it, far above our poor power to add or detract. The world will little note, nor long remember what we say here, but it can never forget what they did here. It is for us the living, rather, to be dedicated here to the unfinished work which they who fought here have thus far so nobly advanced. It is rather for us to be here dedicated to the great task remaining before us—that from these honored dead we take increased devotion to that cause for which they gave the last full measure of devotion; that we here highly resolve that these dead shall not have died in vain; that this nation, under God, shall have a new birth of freedom; and that government of the people, by the people, for the people, shall not perish from the earth.

●◆ What is Lincoln's viewpoint in this speech? Do you agree? Explain.

189

The Battle of Gettysburg, which took place in 1863, was one of the bloodiest of the Civil War. Five months after the battle ended, President Lincoln made this address at a dedication ceremony meant to honor the thousands of soldiers who died at Gettysburg. Lincoln delivered this speech to a crowd of people—many of whom were grief-stricken mothers, fathers, and children of the men who died at Gettysburg.

●◆Imagine you are Lincoln. How do you feel once your speech is over? Then imagine you are a member of Lincoln's audience. How do you feel about his speech? Write a diary entry that reflects Lincoln's viewpoint and a diary entry that reflects the viewpoint of a member of his audience.

Lincoln	Member of his audience

190

Two
Tone

The author's tone in a piece of persuasive writing can give you clues about the author's viewpoint. **Tone** reflects a writer's attitude toward his or her subject matter. An author of a persuasive piece uses tone as a way of convincing you, the reader, to adopt his or her viewpoint. Paying attention to the tone of a persuasive piece can help you understand the message the author has for you. For example, think of the formal, solemn tone ("Four score and seven years ago…") of Lincoln's Gettysburg Address. Lincoln purposely adopted this tone to show how grieved he was about the loss of life—and how desperate he was for the war to end.

As you read Martin Luther King, Jr.'s "I Have a Dream" speech, think about the tone. Circle the words and phrases that help create this tone.

"I Have a Dream" by Martin Luther King, Jr.

Response notes

Five score years ago, a great American, in whose symbolic shadow we stand, signed the Emancipation Proclamation. This momentous decree came as a great beacon light of hope to millions of Negro slaves who had been seared in the flames of withering injustice. It came as a joyous daybreak to end the long night of captivity.

But one hundred years later, we must face the tragic fact that the Negro is still not free. One hundred years later, the life of the Negro is still sadly crippled by the manacles of segregation and the chains of discrimination. One hundred years later, the Negro lives on a lonely island of poverty in the midst of a vast ocean of material prosperity. One hundred years later, the Negro is still languishing in the corners of American society and finds himself an exile in his own land. So we have come here today to dramatize an appalling condition.

In a sense we have come to our nation's Capitol to cash a check. When the architects of our republic wrote the magnificent words of the Constitution and the Declaration of Independence, they were signing a promissory note to which every American was to fall heir. This note was a promise that all men would be guaranteed the unalienable rights of life, liberty, and the pursuit of happiness.

It is obvious today that America has defaulted on this promissory note insofar as her citizens of color are concerned. Instead of honoring this sacred obligation, America has given the Negro people a bad check; a check which has come back marked "insufficient funds." But we refuse to believe that the bank of justice is bankrupt. We refuse to believe that there are

Response notes

insufficient funds in the great vaults of opportunity of this nation. So we have come to cash this check—a check that will give us upon demand the riches of freedom and the security of justice. We have also come to this hallowed spot to remind America of the fierce urgency of *now*. This is no time to engage in the luxury of cooling off or to take the tranquilizing drug of gradualism. *Now* is the time to make real the promises of Democracy. *Now* is the time to rise from the dark and desolate valley of segregation to the sunlit path of racial justice. *Now* is the time to open the doors of opportunity to all of God's children. *Now* is the time to lift our nation from the quicksands of racial injustice to the solid rock of brotherhood.

It would be fatal for the nation to overlook the urgency of the moment and to underestimate the determination of the Negro. This sweltering summer of the Negro's legitimate discontent will not pass until there is an invigorating autumn of freedom and equality. 1963 is not an end, but a beginning. Those who hope that the Negro needed to blow off steam and will now be content will have a rude awakening if the nation returns to business as usual. There will be neither rest nor tranquility in America until the Negro is granted his citizenship rights. The whirlwinds of revolt will continue to shake the foundations of our nation until the bright day of justice emerges.

But there is something that I must say to my people who stand on the warm threshold which leads into the palace of justice. In the process of gaining our rightful place we must not be guilty of wrongful deeds. Let us not seek to satisfy our thirst for freedom by drinking from the cup of bitterness and hatred. We must forever conduct our struggle on the high plane of dignity and discipline. We must not allow our creative protest to degenerate into physical violence. Again and again we must rise to the majestic heights of meeting physical force with soul force. The marvelous new militancy which has engulfed the Negro community must not lead us to a distrust of all white people, for many of our white brothers, as evidenced by their presence here today, have come to realize that their destiny is tied up with our destiny and their freedom is inextricably bound to our freedom. We cannot walk alone.

And as we walk, we must make the pledge that we shall march ahead. We cannot turn back. There are those who are asking the devotees of civil rights, "When will you be satisfied?" We can never be satisfied as long as the Negro is the victim of the unspeakable horrors of police brutality. We can never be satisfied as long as our bodies, heavy with the fatigue of travel, cannot gain lodging in the motels of the

"I Have a Dream" by Martin Luther King, Jr.

Response notes

highways and the hotels of the cities. We cannot be satisfied as long as the Negro's basic mobility is from a smaller ghetto to a larger one. We can never be satisfied as long as a Negro in Mississippi cannot vote and a Negro in New York believes he has nothing for which to vote. No, no, we are not satisfied, and we will not be satisfied until justice rolls down like waters and righteousness like a mighty stream.

I am not unmindful that some of you have come here out of great trials and tribulations. Some of you have come fresh from narrow jail cells. Some of you have come from areas where your quest for freedom left you battered by the storms of persecution and staggered by the winds of police brutality. You have been the veterans of creative suffering. Continue to work with the faith that unearned suffering is redemptive.

Go back to Mississippi, go back to Alabama, go back to South Carolina, go back to Georgia, go back to Louisiana, go back to the slums and ghettos of our northern cities, knowing that somehow this situation can and will be changed. Let us not wallow in the valley of despair.

I say to you today, my friends, that in spite of the difficulties and frustrations of the moment I still have a dream. It is a dream deeply rooted in the American dream.

I have a dream that one day this nation will rise up and live out the true meaning of its creed: "We hold these truths to be self-evident; that all men are created equal."

I have a dream that one day on the red hills of Georgia the sons of former slaves and the sons of former slaveowners will be able to sit down together at the table of brotherhood.

I have a dream that the state of Mississippi, a desert state, sweltering with the heat of injustice and oppression, will be transformed into an oasis of freedom and justice.

I have a dream that my four little children will one day live in a nation where they will not be judged by the color of their skin but by the content of their character.

I have a dream today.

I have a dream that the state of Alabama, whose governor's lips are presently dripping with the words of interposition and nullification, will be transformed into a situation where little black boys and black girls will be able to join hands with little white boys and white girls and walk together as sisters and brothers.

I have a dream today.

I have a dream that one day every valley shall be exalted, every hill and mountain shall be made low, the rough places will be made plain, and the crooked places will be made straight, and the glory of the Lord shall be revealed, and all flesh shall see it together.

193

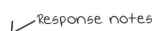

"I Have a Dream" by Martin Luther King

This is our hope. This is the faith with which I return to the South. With this faith we will be able to hew out of the mountain of despair a stone of hope. With this faith we will be able to transform the jangling discords of our nation into a beautiful symphony of brotherhood. With this faith we will be able to work together, to pray together, to struggle together, to go to jail together, to stand up for freedom together, knowing that we will be free one day.

This will be the day when all of God's children will be able to sing with new meaning, "My country, 'tis of thee, sweet land of liberty, of thee I sing. Land where my fathers died, land of the pilgrims' pride, from every mountainside, let freedom ring."

And if America is to be a great nation this must become true. So let freedom ring from the prodigious hilltops of New Hampshire. Let freedom ring from the mighty mountains of New York. Let freedom ring from the heightening Alleghenies of Pennsylvania!

Let freedom ring from the snowcapped Rockies of Colorado!

Let freedom ring from the curvaceous peaks of California!

But not only that; let freedom ring from Stone Mountain of Georgia!

Let freedom ring from Lookout Mountain of Tennessee!

Let freedom ring from every hill and molehill of Mississippi. From every mountainside, let freedom ring.

When we let freedom ring, when we let it ring from every village and every hamlet, from every state and every city, we will be able to speed up that day when all of God's children, black men and white men, Jews and Gentiles, Protestants and Catholics, will be able to join hands and sing in the words of the old Negro spiritual, "Free at last! free at last! thank God Almighty, we are free at last!"

●◆ In the space below, reflect on your reaction to King's speech.

....

....

....

....

●◆ What three words would you use to describe King's tone?

....

194

●◆Use this graphic organizer to help you compare the tone of King's speech to the tone of Lincoln's Gettysburg Address.

King

Tone:

....

....

Viewpoint:

|||||||||||||||||||||||||||||||||||||||||||||||||||||||

....

....

....

....

Lincoln

Tone:

....

....

Viewpoint:

....

....

....

....

195

●◆Reflect briefly on how the tone of each speech provides clues about the speaker's viewpoint. Then describe how the tone of each speech makes you—the reader—feel.

....

....

|||||||||||||||||||||||||||||||||||||||||||||||||||||||||||||||||||||||

....

....

....

....

An author's tone can often give clues about the author's message and his or her feelings about the subject.

Word choice is an important aspect of a persuasive writer's craft. Every word is important in an argument, because each word represents a fresh opportunity to convince the audience.

Notice Lincoln's careful use of such words as *altogether fitting and proper, consecrate,* and *hallow.* Words like these brought a dignity to the occasion that Lincoln knew he needed. Think about how different his speech would have been if had he used "Eighty-seven" instead of "Four score and seven" or "it's a really good idea to do this" instead of "it is altogether fitting and proper that we should do this." Because his words had a dignified sound to them, he was able to persuade his audience to remain dignified and strong during extremely trying and difficult times.

●◆Look at this paragraph from Dr. King's speech. Circle words and phrases that stand out. Then rewrite the paragraph using different words to convey the same basic meaning as the original.

I am not unmindful that some of you have come here out of great trials and tribulations. Some of you have come fresh from narrow jail cells. Some of you have come from areas where your quest for freedom left you battered by the storms of persecution and staggered by the winds of police brutality. You have been the veterans of creative suffering. Continue to work with the faith that unearned suffering is redemptive.

My rewrite

●◆Explain how the changes you made to this paragraph change the "feel" of King's speech.

●◆Does your rewrite change the effectiveness of King's speech? Explain.

Persuasive writers know that word choice contributes to the effectiveness of an argument.

There are many different ways to support an argument. One effective technique is to offer your own personal experiences as evidence for your viewpoint. When you use your personal experiences as support, your **audience** may be reminded of their own experiences and therefore have an easier time connecting with what you say.

Read this speech by Robert F. Kennedy, the brother of John F. Kennedy. Watch for places in the speech where Kennedy refers to his own experiences.

← Response notes

"On the Death of Martin Luther King, Jr." by Robert F. Kennedy

I have bad news for you, for all of our fellow citizens, and people who love peace all over the world, and that is that Martin Luther King was shot and killed tonight.

Martin Luther King dedicated his life to love and to justice for his fellow human beings, and he died because of that effort.

In this difficult day, in this difficult time for the United States, it is perhaps well to ask what kind of a nation we are and what direction we want to move in. For those of you who are black—considering the evidence there evidently is that there were white people who were responsible—you can be filled with bitterness, with hatred, and with a desire for revenge. We can move in that direction as a country, in great polarization—black people amongst black, white people amongst white, filled with hatred toward one another.

Or we can make an effort, as Martin Luther King did, to understand and to comprehend, and to replace that violence, that stain of bloodshed that has spread across our land, with an effort to understand with compassion and love.

For those of you who are black and are tempted to be filled with hatred and distrust at the injustice of such an act, against all white people, I can only say that I feel in my own heart the same kind of feeling. I had a member of my family killed, but he was killed by a white man. But we have to make an effort in the United States, we have to make an effort to understand, to go beyond these rather difficult times.

My favorite poet was Aeschylus. He wrote: "In our sleep, pain which cannot forget falls drop by drop upon the heart until, in our own despair, against our will, comes wisdom through the awful grace of God."

What we need in the United States is not division; what we need in the United States is not hatred; what we need in the United States is not violence or lawlessness, but love and wisdom, and compassion toward one another, and a feeling of justice towards those who still suffer within our country, whether they be white or they be black.

"On the Death of Martin Luther King, Jr." by Robert F. Kennedy

So I shall ask you tonight to return home, to say a prayer for the family of Martin Luther King, that's true, but more importantly to say a prayer for our own country, which all of us love—a prayer for understanding and that compassion of which I spoke.

We can do well in this country. We will have difficult times. We've had difficult times in the past. We will have difficult times in the future. It is not the end of violence; it is not the end of lawlessness; it is not the end of disorder.

But the vast majority of white people and the vast majority of black people in this country want to live together, want to improve the quality of our life, and want justice for all human beings who abide in our land.

Let us dedicate ourselves to what the Greeks wrote so many years ago: to tame the savageness of man and to make gentle the life of this world.

Let us dedicate ourselves to that, and say a prayer for our country and for our people.

●◆ **What is your opinion of Kennedy's speech? Explain.**

199

....

....

....

....

....

....

●◆ **Give three examples of how Kennedy uses his own experiences to support his argument.**

1. ....

2. ....

3. ....

●◆Imagine you are one of Robert Kennedy's advisors. Kennedy is planning to rewrite this speech so that he can give it on national TV. Write a memo to Kennedy. In your memo, evaluate the effectiveness of his argument. Tell him whether he needs *more*, *less*, or *different* support for his argument. Then explain why.

MEMORANDUM

To: Robert Kennedy
From:
Re: Your Speech

Persuasive writers often use personal experiences as support for their arguments. Readers often find it easy to relate to these "real" stories.

Five Brainstorming

Another effective persuasive technique is *brainstorming*. Brainstorming involves addressing your readers directly to give them the impression that they are "equal partners" with you in your quest to right a wrong, find a solution, or make a statement.

Brainstorming is a particularly effective technique because it makes the reader (or listener) feel involved and important. When you brainstorm, you say in essence: "I'm not going to *tell* you what to do. You and I are going to work through this problem together."

Consider how Robert Kennedy uses brainstorming in "On the Death of Martin Luther King, Jr.":

In this difficult day, in this difficult time for the United States, it is perhaps well to ask what kind of a nation we are and what direction we want to move in. For those of you who are black—considering the evidence there evidently is that there were white people who were responsible—you can be filled with bitterness, with hatred, and with a desire for revenge. We can move in that direction as a country, in great polarization—black people amongst black, white people amongst white, filled with hatred toward one another.

Or we can make an effort, as Martin Luther King did, to understand and to comprehend, and to replace that violence, that stain of bloodshed that has spread across our land, with an effort to understand with compassion and love.

Return to the whole of Kennedy's speech. **Highlight** other places he seems to be brainstorming with his audience.

●◆ Why do you think Kennedy relied so heavily on brainstorming in this speech?

●◆ What do you think of this persuasive technique?

201

●◆ Now plan a persuasive speech of your own. Use brainstorming as your persuasive technique. Begin by choosing a topic from the list below.

POSSIBLE TOPICS

- Home schooling
- Mandatory community service for high school students
- Other: ....

- Raising the voting age to 21
- Year-round school
- Weekend/Vacation Homework

●◆ Jot down some notes to prepare for your speech. Decide on the points you will make to persuade your audience.

My topic: ....

My argument: ....

Points I want to make: ....

- ....

202

- ....

- ....

- ....

●◆ Choose one or two points from your notes. Write a paragraph in which you use *brainstorming* to persuade your audience to agree with your points.

....

....

....

....

....

....

When you read persuasive writing, look for the use of brainstorming. Persuasive writers often use this technique to help readers feel involved in the argument.

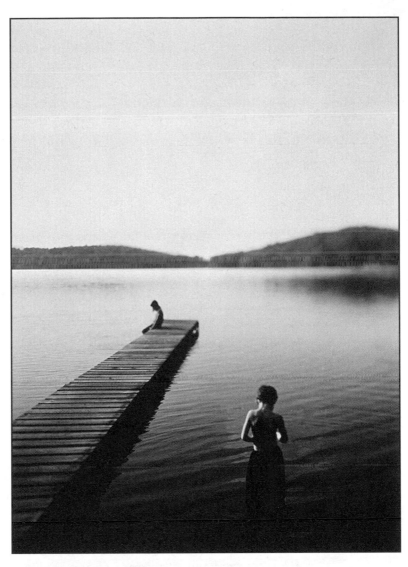

Focus on the Writer: Mark Twain

Humor must not professedly teach, and it must not professedly preach, but it must do both if it would live forever.

—Mark Twain

Mark Twain, born Samuel Langhorne Clemens, did not initially plan to write humorous works. In fact, writing was not even his first career choice. After ending his formal schooling early, he learned the printing trade and eventually fulfilled his dream of becoming a steamboat pilot on the Mississippi River. When the Civil War ended river trade, Twain turned to writing as a career. Twain's lifetime, from 1835–1910, spanned an era of tremendous changes in the United States in politics, technology, and society. Twain's works indirectly commented on these aspects of life. He used humor as a means both to entertain and to teach.

One Early Attempts at Humor

During eighth grade, Mark Twain left school and became an apprentice on his uncle's newspaper. Even in his early "newspaper days," Twain showed a flair for humorous writing. In this excerpt, Twain tells about the newspaper articles he wrote—at the age of thirteen—for a small weekly paper in Hannibal, Missouri. As you read, think about what this excerpt reveals about Twain and the kind of person he was. How did he use humor to entertain others?

←Response notes→

from **"My First Literary Venture"** by Mark Twain

I was a very smart child at the age of thirteen—an unusually smart child, I thought at the time. It was then that I did my first newspaper scribbling, and most unexpectedly to me it stirred up a fine sensation in the community. It did, indeed, and I was very proud of it, too. I was a printer's "devil," and a progressive and aspiring one. My uncle had me on his paper (the *Weekly Hannibal Journal,* two dollars a year in advance—five hundred subscribers, and they paid in cordwood, cabbages, and unmarketable turnips), and on a lucky summer's day he left town to be gone a week, and asked me if I thought I could edit one issue of the paper judiciously. Ah! didn't I want to try! Higgins was the editor on the rival paper. He had lately been jilted, and one night a friend found an open note on the poor fellow's bed, in which he stated that he could not longer endure life and had drowned himself in Bear Creek. The friend ran down there and discovered Higgins wading back to shore. He had concluded he wouldn't. The village was full of it for several days, but Higgins did not suspect it. I thought this was a fine opportunity. I wrote an elaborately wretched account of the whole matter, and then illustrated it with villainous cuts engraved on the bottoms of wooden type with a jackknife—one of them a picture of Higgins wading out into the creek in his shirt, with a lantern, sounding the depth of the water with a walking-stick. I thought it was desperately funny, and was densely unconscious that there was any <u>moral obliquity</u> about such a publication. Being satisfied with this effort I looked around for other worlds to conquer, and it struck me that it would make good, interesting matter to charge the editor of a neighboring country paper with a piece of gratuitous rascality and "see him squirm."

I did it, putting the article into the form of a parody on the "Burial of Sir John Moore"—and a pretty crude parody it was, too.

Then I <u>lampooned</u> two prominent citizens outrageously—not because they had done anything to deserve, but merely because I thought it was my duty to make the paper lively.

lack of moral judgment

ridiculed in writing

●◆Do you think Mark Twain did the right thing by printing these articles in the newspaper? Imagine that you are Twain's uncle, back from vacation. What would you say to Twain about his printing these articles?

Continue reading the excerpt to find out what happened after the articles appeared in the newspaper.

from **"My First Literary Venture"** by Mark Twain

205

Response notes

For once the *Hannibal Journal* was in demand—a novelty it had not experienced before. The whole town was stirred. Higgins dropped in with a double-barreled shotgun early in the forenoon. When he found that it was an infant (as he called me) that had done him the damage, he simply pulled my ears and went away; but he threw up his situation that night and left town for good. The tailor came with his goose and a pair of shears; but he despised me, too, and departed for the South that night. The two lampooned citizens came with threats of libel, and went away incensed at my insignificance. The country editor pranced in with a war-whoop next day, suffering for blood to drink; but he ended by forgiving me cordially and inviting me down to the drug store to wash away all animosity in a friendly bumper of "Fahnestock's Vermifuge." It was his little joke. My uncle was very angry when he got back— unreasonably so, I thought, considering what an impetus I had given the paper, and considering also that gratitude for his preservation ought to have been uppermost in his mind, inasmuch as by his delay he had so wonderfully escaped dissection, tomahawking, libel, and getting his head shot off. But he softened when he looked at the accounts and saw that I had actually booked the unparalleled number of thirty-three new subscribers, and had the vegetables to show for it, cordwood, cabbage, beans, and unsalable turnips enough to run the family for two years!

●◆ Were you surprised by how people reacted to Twain's humor? Why or why not?

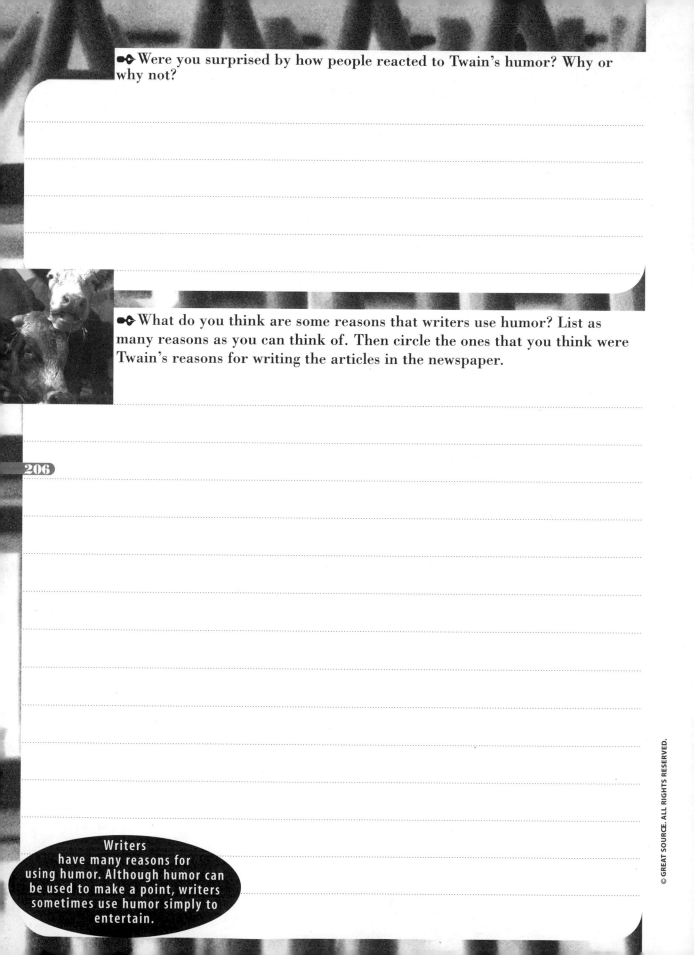

●◆ What do you think are some reasons that writers use humor? List as many reasons as you can think of. Then circle the ones that you think were Twain's reasons for writing the articles in the newspaper.

206

Writers have many reasons for using humor. Although humor can be used to make a point, writers sometimes use humor simply to entertain.

Two Exaggeration

Although Mark Twain was an experienced riverboat pilot himself, he at one point took a "field trip" on a riverboat in order to write about life on the Mississippi River. His book, *Life on the Mississippi*, is a mixture of stories, folk tales, quotes from travelers, and Twain's up-and-down enthusiasm for the boats.

In this excerpt, Twain describes a conversation he had with a riverboat pilot who was skilled in "the noble art of inflating his facts." Twain kept his identity hidden from the pilot during the interview, acting as if he knew nothing about the river. As you read the excerpt, put an "X" near parts that you think are *exaggerations*—statements that make things greater than they really are or that overstate the truth.

from *Life on the Mississippi* by Mark Twain

Response notes

Once, when an odd-looking craft, with a vast coal-scuttle slanting aloft on the end of a beam, was steaming by in the distance, he indifferently drew attention to it, as one might to an object grown wearisome through familiarity, and observed that it was an "alligator boat."

"An alligator boat? What's it for?"

"To dredge out alligators with."

"Are they so thick as to be troublesome?"

"Well, not now, because the Government keeps them down. But they used to be. Not everywhere; but in favorite places, here and there, where the river is wide and <u>shoal</u>—like Plum Point, and Stack Island, and so on—places they call alligator beds."

shallow

"Did they actually impede navigation?"

"Years ago, yes, in very low water; there was hardly a trip, then, that we didn't get aground on alligators."

It seemed to me that I should certainly have to get out my tomahawk. However, I restrained myself and said—

"It must have been dreadful."

"Yes, it was one of the main difficulties about piloting. It was so hard to tell anything about the water; the damned things shift around so—never lie still five minutes at a time. You can tell a wind-reef, straight off, by the look of it; you can tell a break; you can tell a sand-reef—that's all easy; but an alligator reef doesn't show up, worth anything. Nine times in ten you can't tell where the water is; and when you *do* see where it is, like as not it ain't there when *you* get there, the devils have swapped around so, meantime. Of course there were some few pilots that could judge of alligator water nearly as well as they could of any other kind, but they had to have natural talent for it; it wasn't a thing a body could *learn*, you had to be born with it. Let me see: there was Ben Thornburg, and Beck Jolly, and Squire Bell, and Horace Bixby, and Major Downing, and John Stevenson, and Billy Gordon, and Jim Brady, and George Ealer, and Billy Youngblood—all A 1 alligator pilots. *They* could tell alligator water as far as another Christian could tell whiskey. Read it?—Ah, *couldn't* they, though! I only wish I had as many dollars as they could read alligator water a mile and a half off. Yes, and it paid them to do it, too. A good alligator pilot could always get fifteen hundred dollars a month. Nights, other people had to lay up for alligators, but those fellows never laid up for alligators; they never laid up for anything but fog. They could *smell* the best alligator water—so it was said; I don't know whether it was so or not, and I think a body's got his hands full enough if he sticks to just what he knows himself, without going around backing up other people's say-so's, though there's a plenty that ain't backward about doing it, as long as they can roust out something wonderful to tell. Which is not the style of Robert Styles, by as much as three fathom—maybe quarter-*less*."

[My! Was this Rob Styles?—This mustached and stately figure?—A slim enough cub, in my time. How he has improved in comeliness in five-and-twenty years—and in the noble art of inflating his facts.] After these musings, I said aloud—

"I should think that dredging out the alligators wouldn't have done much good, because they could come back again right away."

"If you had had as much experience of alligators as I have, you wouldn't talk like that. You dredge an alligator once and he's *convinced*. It's the last you hear of *him*. He wouldn't come back for pie. If there's one thing that an alligator is more down on than another, it's being dredged. Besides, they were not simply shoved out of the way; the most of the scoopful were scooped aboard; they emptied them into the hold; and when they had got a trip, they took them to Orleans to the Government works."

"What for?"

"Why, to make soldier-shoes out of their hides. All the Government shoes are made of alligator hide. It makes the best shoes in the world. They last five years, and they won't absorb water. The alligator fishery is a Government monopoly. All the alligators are Government property—just like the live-oaks. You cut down a live-oak, and Government fines you fifty dollars; you kill an alligator, and up you go for misprision of treason—lucky duck if they don't hang you, too. And they will,

illegal act against the government

208

from *Life on the Mississippi* by Mark Twain

if you're a Democrat. The buzzard is the sacred bird of the South, and you can't touch him; the alligator is the sacred bird of the Government, and you've got to let him alone."

"Do you ever get aground on the alligators now?"

"Oh, no! It hasn't happened for years."

"Well, then, why do they still keep the alligator boats in service?"

"Just for police duty—nothing more. They merely go up and down now and then. The present generation of alligators know them as easy as a burglar knows a <u>roundsman;</u> when they see one coming, they break camp and go for the woods."

policeman

●◆ How believable is the pilot's story about alligator boats? What exactly does the pilot exaggerate?

....

....

....

....

●◆ What is the effect of Twain's use of exaggeration? What do you think of the pilot after hearing his story?

....

....

....

....

....

....

....

....

> Authors use exaggeration not only to entertain and add humor, but also to give insights into characters.

Satire involves using sarcasm, humor, or exaggeration to ridicule or make fun of human vice or weakness, often with the intent of correcting, or changing, the subject of the satiric attack. *A Connecticut Yankee in King Arthur's Court* is a satire Mark Twain wrote to poke fun at a variety of things, including "Yankee know-how." The narrator of the story is hit on the head and transported from 1800s Hartford, Connecticut, to Medieval England. There, his ingenuity and knowledge of technology shock and amaze the people. In this excerpt, he is preparing to fight some monsters who have overrun a castle. But first he has to get dressed.

Response notes

from ***A Connecticut Yankee in King Arthur's Court***
by Mark Twain

I was to have an early breakfast, and start at dawn, for that was the usual way; but I had the demon's own time with my armor, and this delayed me a little. It is troublesome to get into, and there is so much detail. First you wrap a layer or two of blanket around your body, for a sort of cushion and to keep off the cold iron; then you put on your sleeves and shirt of chain mail—these are made of small steel links woven together, and they form a fabric so flexible that if you toss your shirt onto the floor, it slumps into a pile like a peck of wet fish-net; it is very heavy and is nearly the uncomfortablest material in the world for a nightshirt, yet plenty used it for that—tax-collectors, and reformers, and one-horse kings with a defective title, and those sorts of people; then you put on your shoes—flatboats roofed over with interleaving bands of steel—and screw your clumsy spurs into the heels. Next you buckle your greaves on your legs, and your cuisses on your thighs; then come your backplate and your breastplate, and you begin to feel crowded; then you hitch onto the breast-plate the half-petticoat of broad overlapping bands of steel which hangs down in front but is scolloped out behind so you can sit down, and isn't any real improvement on an inverted coal-scuttle, either for looks or for wear, or to wipe your hands on; next you belt on your sword; then you put your stove-pipe joints onto your arms, your iron gauntlets onto your hands, your iron rat-trap onto your head, with a rag of steel web hitched onto it to hang over the back of your neck—and there you are, snug as a candle in a candle-mold. There is no time to dance. Well, a man that is packed away like that is a nut that isn't worth the cracking, there is so little of the meat, when you get down to it, by comparison with the shell.

The boys helped me, or I never could have got in. Just as

from *A Connecticut Yankee in King Arthur's Court*
by Mark Twain

Response notes

we finished, Sir Bedivere happened in, and I saw that as like as not I hadn't chosen the most convenient outfit for a long trip. How stately he looked; and tall and broad and grand. He had on his head a conical steel casque that only came down to his ears, and for visor had only a narrow steel bar that extended down to his upper lip and protected his nose; and all the rest of him, from neck to heel, was flexible chain mail, trousers and all. But pretty much all of him was hidden under his outside garment, which of course was of chain mail, as I said, and hung straight from his shoulders to his ankles; and from his middle to the bottom, both before and behind, was divided, so that he could ride and let the skirts hang down on each side. He was going grailing, and it was just the outfit for it, too. I would have given a good deal for that ulster, but it was too late now to be fooling around. The sun was just up, the king and the court were all on hand to see me off and wish me luck; so it wouldn't be etiquette for me to tarry. You don't get on your horse yourself; no, if you tried it you would get disappointed. They carry you out, just as they carry a sun-struck man to the drug store, and put you on, and help get you to rights, and fix your feet in the stirrups; and all the while you do feel so strange and stuffy and like somebody else—like somebody that has been married on a sudden, or struck by lightning, or something like that, and hasn't quite fetched around yet, and is sort of numb, and can't just get his bearings. Then they stood up the mast they called a spear, in its socket by my left foot, and I gripped it with my hand; lastly they hung my shield around my neck, and I was all complete and ready to up anchor and get to sea. Everybody was as good to me as they could be, and a maid of honor gave me the stirrup-cup her own self. There was nothing more to do now, but for that damsel to get up behind me on a pillion, which she did, and put an arm or so around me to hold on. And so we started, and everybody gave us a good-by and waved their handkerchiefs or helmets. And everybody we met, going down the hill and through the village, was respectful to us, except some shabby little boys on the outskirts. They said:

"Oh, what a guy!" And hove clods at us.

In my experience boys are the same in all ages. They don't respect anything, they don't care for anything or anybody. They say "Go up, baldhead" to the prophet going his unoffending way in the gray of antiquity; they sass me in the holy gloom of the Middle Ages; and I had seen them act the same way in Buchanan's administration; I remember, because I

from *A Connecticut Yankee in King Arthur's Court*
by Mark Twain

was there and helped. The prophet had his bears and settled with his boys; and I wanted to get down and settle with mine, but it wouldn't answer, because I couldn't have got up again.
I hate a country without a <u>derrick</u>.

hangman's
gallows

➽ What point do you think Twain is trying to make? How does he use humor to make this point?

....

....

....

....

➽ What sentences or phrases strike you as humorous? List two or three examples and explain what they make fun of or satirize.

....

....

....

....

....

....

....

....

When you come across satire in your reading, keep in mind that its purpose is to ridicule or convey amusement to make a point or affect change.

Four
Humor in Character

In *The Adventures of Huckleberry Finn*, Twain uses humor to show the inhumanity of slavery through Huckleberry Finn's attempts to help a runaway slave. Huckleberry serves as the narrator of the story. As you read this excerpt from the beginning of the book, jot down your ideas about what Huck Finn is like.

from *The Adventures of Huckleberry Finn* by Mark Twain

Response notes

You don't know about me, without you have read a book by the name of "The Adventures of Tom Sawyer," but that ain't no matter. That book was made by Mr. Mark Twain, and he told the truth, mainly. There was things which he stretched, but mainly he told the truth. That is nothing. I never seen anybody but lied, one time or another, without it was Aunt Polly, or the widow, or maybe Mary. Aunt Polly—Tom's Aunt Polly, she is—and Mary, and the Widow Douglas, is all told about in that book—which is mostly a true book; with some stretchers, as I said before.

Now the way that the book winds up, is this: Tom and me found the money that the robbers hid in the cave, and it made us rich. We got six thousand dollars apiece—all gold. It was an awful sight of money when it was piled up. Well, Judge Thatcher, he took it and put it out at interest, and it fetched us a dollar a day apiece, all the year round—more than a body could tell what to do with. The Widow Douglas, she took me for her son, and allowed she would civilize me; but it was rough living in the house all the time, considering how dismal regular and decent the widow was in all her ways; and so when I couldn't stand it no longer, I lit out. I got into my old rags, and my sugar-hogshead again, and was free and satisfied. But Tom Sawyer, he hunted me up and said he was going to start a band of robbers, and I might join if I would go back to the widow and be respectable. So I went back.

The widow she cried over me, and called me a poor lost lamb, and she called me a lot of other names, too, but she never meant no harm by it. She put me in them new clothes again, and I couldn't do nothing but sweat and sweat, and feel all cramped up. Well, then, the old thing commenced again. The widow rung a bell for supper, and you had to come to time. When you got to the table you couldn't go right to eating, but you had to wait for the widow to tuck down her head and grumble a little over the victuals, though there warn't really

213

Response notes

anything the matter with them. That is, nothing only everything was cooked by itself. In a barrel of odds and ends it is different; things get mixed up, and the juice kind of swaps around, and the things go better.

After supper she got out her book and learned me about Moses and the Bulrushers; and I was in a sweat to find out all about him; but by-and-by she let it out that Moses had been dead a considerable long time; so then I didn't care no more about him; because I don't take no stock in dead people.

Pretty soon I wanted to smoke, and asked the widow to let me. But she wouldn't. She said it was a mean practice and wasn't clean, and I must try to not do it any more. That is just the way with some people. They get down on a thing when they don't know nothing about it. Here she was a bothering about Moses, which was no kin to her, and no use to anybody, being gone, you see, yet finding a power of fault with me for doing a thing that had some good in it. And she took snuff too; of course that was all right, because she done it herself.

Her sister, Miss Watson, a tolerable slim old maid, with goggles on, had just come to live with her, and took a set at me now, with a spelling-book. She worked me middling hard for about an hour, and then the widow made her ease up. I couldn't stood it much longer. Then for an hour it was deadly dull, and I was fidgety. Miss Watson would say, "Don't put your feet up there, Huckleberry;" and "Don't scrunch up like that, Huckleberry—set up straight;" and pretty soon she would say, "Don't gap and stretch like that, Huckleberry—why don't you try to behave?" Then she told me all about the bad place, and I said I wished I was there. She got mad, then, but I didn't mean no harm. All I wanted was to go somewheres; all I wanted was a change, I warn't particular. She said it was wicked to say what I said; said she wouldn't say it for the whole world; *she* was going to live so as to go to the good place. Well, I couldn't see no advantage in going where she was going, so I made up my mind I wouldn't try for it. But I never said so, because it would only make trouble, and wouldn't do no good.

214

One of the strengths of the novel is its humor. Huck tells things that are funny in a very matter-of-fact way, not knowing himself that they are funny. What do you think is humorous about Huck and his situation? Go back to the excerpt and mark parts that you think are amusing. Share your ideas with a partner.

What kind of person is Huckleberry Finn? Think about how he feels about himself, how he feels about education, and how he relates to other people.

Look back at your description of Huck. How does Twain's use of humor affect your perception of the character? Would you think the same of Huck if he didn't tell his story so humorously? Explain.

215

Writers can use humor to reveal what characters are like.

Twain was, literally, a man of letters. He wrote them to family members, to friends, to other writers, and he even had the job of writing letters to a newspaper "back home" during a trip he took to Hawaii. By looking at his letters, we can get a glimpse of Twain's sense of humor—sometimes gentle, sometimes biting and sarcastic, sometimes full of wisdom or wild exaggerations. These two letters show two different facets of Twain's personality. As you read them, jot down your thoughts about Twain.

Readers and critics alike enjoyed Mark Twain's novel *The Adventures of Huckleberry Finn*. Sales of the novel were brisk. But not everyone approved of the book, and some libraries and stores censored it. Twain wrote this letter to his publisher, Charles L. Webster, to tell about an instance of censorship.

Response notes

To Chas. L. Webster, in New York:

Mch 18, '85
Dear Charley,—The Committee of the Public Library of Concord, Mass., have given us a rattling tip-top puff which will go into every paper in the country. They have expelled Huck from their library as "trash and suitable only for the slums." That will sell 25,000 copies for us sure.

Ys
S.L.C.

During his childhood, Mark Twain always owned at least one cat. As an adult, he usually had a cat beside him as he worked. In this letter, he tells a woman who had previously written to him about one of his favorite cats and a game the cat plays.

To Mrs. Mabel Larkin Patterson, in Chicago:
Redding, Connecticut,

Oct. 2, '08.
Dear Mrs. Patterson,—The contents of your letter are very pleasant and very welcome, and I thank you for them, sincerely. If I can find a photograph of my "Tammany" and her kittens, I will enclose it in this. One of them likes to be crammed into a corner-pocket of the billiard table, which he fits as snugly as does a finger in a glove and then he watches the game (and obstructs it) by the hour, and spoils many a shot by putting out his paw and changing the direction of a passing ball. Whenever a ball is in his arms, or so close to him that it cannot be played upon without risk of hurting him, the player is privileged to remove it to any one of the 3 spots that chances to be vacant.

Ah, no, my lecturing days are over for good and all.

Sincerely yours,
S. L. Clemens

●❖ What do these letters reveal about Twain? Explain.

Humor must not professedly teach, and it must not professedly preach, but it must do both if it would live forever.

—Mark Twain

●◆ This quotation from Mark Twain appeared at the beginning of the unit. How well does Twain achieve his goal about using humor in his writing? Choose one of the pieces in this unit and show how it does—or does not—use humor to teach something to readers without "preaching."

218

Personal letters can provide insights into a writer, both through their subject matter and their tone.

Texts

10 "Alabama Earth" from *Collected Poems* by Langston Hughes. Copyright © 1994 by the Estate of Langston Hughes. Reprinted by permission of Alfred A. Knopf Inc.

11 "Theme for English B" from *Collected Poems* by Langston Hughes. Copyright © 1994 by the Estate of Langston Hughes. Reprinted by permission of Alfred A. Knopf Inc.

13 "Aunt Sue's Stories" from *Collected Poems* by Langston Hughes. Copyright © 1994 by the Estate of Langston Hughes. Reprinted by permission of Alfred A. Knopf Inc.

15 "The Weary Blues" from *Collected Poems* by Langston Hughes. Copyright © 1994 by the Estate of Langston Hughes. Reprinted by permission of Alfred A. Knopf Inc.

17 "Simple Arithmetic" from *The Return of Simple* by Langston Hughes, edited by Akiba Sullivan Harper. Copyright © 1994 by Ramona Bass and Arnold Rampersad. Reprinted by permission of Hill and Wang, a division of Farrar, Straus & Giroux, Inc.

20 Excerpt from "Less than Lyric" from *I Wonder As I Wander* by Langston Hughes, introduction by Arnold Rampersad. Copyright © 1956 by Langston Hughes. Copyright renewed © 1984 by George Houston Bass, copyright introduction © 1993 by Arnold Rampersad. Reprinted by permission of Hill and Wang, a division of Farrar, Straus & Giroux, Inc.

24, 29 from *I Know Why the Caged Bird Sings* by Maya Angelou. Copyright © 1969 and renewed 1997 by Maya Angelou. Reprinted by permission of Random House, Inc.

32 from *Now Is Your Time!* Copyright © 1991 by Walter Dean Myers. Used by permission of HarperCollins Publishers.

37 "Like Bookends" from *If Only I Could Tell You* by Eve Merriam. Copyright © 1983 by Eve Merriam. Reprinted by permission of Marian Reiner.

40 from *Journey to Topaz* by Yoshiko Uchida. Copyright © 1971 by Yoshiko Uchida. Reprinted by permission of the Estate of Yoshiko Uchida.

43 Excerpt from *The Witch of Blackbird Pond*. Copyright © 1958, renewed 1986 by Elizabeth George Speare. Reprinted by permission of Houghton Mifflin Co. All rights reserved.

49 "Those Three Wishes" Copyright © 1982 by Judith Gorog. First appeared in *A Taste For Quiet and Other Disquieting Tales*, published by Philomel Books. Reprinted by permission of Curtis Brown, Ltd.

56 "On Thirty-fourth Street" by Gwendolyn Brooks from *Blacks*, published by Third World Press, Chicago. Copyright, by Gwendolyn Brooks © 1991.

58 "Pete at the Zoo" by Gwendolyn Brooks from *Blacks*, published by Third World Press, Chicago. Copyright, by Gwendolyn Brooks © 1991.

60 "The Princess and the Tin Box" by James Thurber. Copyright ® 1940 by James Thurber. Copyright © renewed 1976 by Helen Thurber and Rosemary A. Thurber. Reprinted by arrangement with Rosemary A. Thurber and the Barbara Hogenson Agency.

63 "A Day's Wait" Reprinted with permission of Scribner, a Division of Simon & Schuster, from *Winner Take Nothing* by Ernest Hemingway. Copyright 1933 Charles Scribner's Sons. Copyright renewed © 1961 by Mary Hemingway.

70 "Simile: Willow and Ginkgo" from *A Sky Full of Poems* by Eve Merriam. Copyright © 1964, 1970, 1973 by Eve Merriam. Reprinted by permission of Marian Reiner.

73 "Scaffolding" from *Poems 1965–1975* by Seamus Heaney. Copyright © 1980 by Seamus Heaney. Reprinted by permission of Farrar, Straus & Giroux, Inc.

75 "Fire and Ice" from: *The Poetry of Robert Frost*, edited by Edward Connery Lathem. Copyright 1936, 1951 by Robert Frost, © 1964 by Lesley Frost Ballantine, Copyright 1923, © 1969 by Henry Holt and Company, Inc., © 1997 by Edward Connery Lathem. Reprinted by permission of Henry Holt and Company, Inc.

78, 83 "Gaston" Reprinted by permission of the Trustees of Leland Stanford Junior University.

88 "Memorial and Recommendations of the Grand Council Fire of American Indians presented to the Hon. William Hale Thompson, December 1, 1927" from "The Background" from *Textbooks and the American Indian* by the American Indian Historical Society, written by Jeannette Henry, edited by Rupert Costo. Copyright © 1970 by the Indian Historian Press.

93 "Silencing the Sound of Music" by Dan Rather. Reprinted with permission.

96 "America The Not-so-Beautiful" from *Not That You Asked* by Andrew A. Rooney. Copyright © 1989 by Essay Publications, Inc. Reprinted by permission of Random House, Inc.

104, 107 from *Missing May* by Cynthia Rylant. Copyright © 1992 by Cynthia Rylant. Reprinted by permission of Orchard Books, New York.

109 "Sandy Jane Meador" from *Soda Jerk* by Cynthia Rylant. Copyright © 1990 by Cynthia Rylant. Reprinted by permission of Orchard Books, New York.

112, 114 from *But I'll Be Back Again* by Cynthia Rylant. Copyright © 1989 by Cynthia Rylant. Reprinted by permission of Orchard Books, New York.

118 Excerpt, as submitted, from *The Autobiography of Eleanor Roosevelt* by Eleanor Roosevelt. Copyright © 1937, 1949, 1958, 1961 by Anna Eleanor Roosevelt. Copyright © 1958 by Curtis Publishing Company. Reprinted by permission of HarperCollins Publishers, Inc.

121 "Because I could not stop for Death" Reprinted by permission of the publishers and the Trustees of Amherst College from *The Poems of Emily Dickinson*, Thomas H. Johnson, ed., Cambridge, Mass.: The Belknap Press of Harvard University Press, Copyright © 1951, 1955, 1979, 1983 by the President and Fellows of Harvard College.

126, 129 "The Elevator" by William Sleator. Copyright © 1989 by William Sleator. All rights reserved. Used by permission.

134 *The 1940s: Decade of Triumph and Trouble* Copyright © 1998 by the New York Times. Reprinted by permission.

138 from *Hiroshima* by John Hersey. Copyright 1946 and renewed 1974 by John Hersey. Reprinted by permission of Alfred A. Knopf Inc.

141, 145 Excerpts and figure from *World History: Continuity & Change*, Grades 9-10 Pupil's Edition, copyright © 1997 by Holt, Rinehart and Winston, reprinted by permission of the publisher.

148 "The Promise" Reprinted with the permission of Simon & Schuster Books for Young Readers, an imprint of Simon & Schuster Children's Publishing Division from *The Good Guys of Baseball* by Terry Egan, Stan Friedmann, and Mike Levine. Copyright © 1997 Terry Egan, Stan Friedmann, and Mike Levine.

151 "Power of the Powerless: A Brother's Lesson" by Christopher de Vinck. Reprinted with permission of the author and *The Wall Street Journal* © 1985 Dow Jones & Company, Inc. All rights reserved.

156 Reprinted with the permission of Simon & Schuster Books for Young Readers, an imprint of Simon & Schuster Children's Publishing Division from *I Have Lived a Thousand Years* by Livia Bitton-Jackson. Copyright © 1997 Livia E. Bitton-Jackson.

162 from *The Pearl* by John Steinbeck. Copyright 1945 by John Steinbeck, © renewed 1973 by Elaine Steinbeck, Thom Steinbeck, and John Steinbeck IV. Used by permission of Viking Penguin, a division of Penguin Putnam Inc.

163 "Skin," an excerpt from "The Story of My Body" from *The Latin Deli: Prose and Poetry* by Judith Ortiz Cofer. Copyright © 1993 by Judith Ortiz Cofer. Reprinted by permission of the publisher, The University of Georgia Press.

167 from *Dear America: I Thought My Soul Would Rise and Fly, The Diary of Patsy, A Freed Slave Girl* by Joyce Hansen. Copyright © 1997 by Joyce Hansen. Reprinted by permission of Scholastic Inc. *Dear America* is a trademark of Scholastic Inc.

170 "1(a", copyright © 1958, 1986, 1991 by the Trustees for the E. E. Cummings Trust, from *Complete Poems: 1904-1962* by E. E. Cummings, edited by George J. Firmage. Reprinted by permission of Liveright Publishing Corporation.

171 "Saying Yes" by Diana Chang. Used by permission of the author.

176 "I'm Nobody" Reprinted by permission of the publishers and the Trustees of Amherst College from *The Poems of Emily Dickinson*, Thomas H. Johnson, ed., Cambridge, Mass.: The Belknap Press of Harvard University Press, Copyright © 1951, 1955, 1979, 1983 by the President and Fellows of Harvard College.

183 Copyright © 1959 by Richard Wright. Published by Arcade Publishing, Inc., New York, NY.

185 "Hannah Armstrong" by Edgar Lee Masters from *Spoon River Anthology* by Edgar Lee Masters. Used by permission of Hilary Masters.

191 "I Have a Dream" reprinted by arrangement with the Heirs to the Estate of Martin Luther King, Jr., c/o Writers House, Inc. as agent for the proprietor. Copyright 1963 by Martin Luther King, Jr., copyright renewed 1991 by Coretta Scott King.

216 Letters of Mark Twain from *Mark Twain's Letters*, edited by Albert Bigelow Paine (Harper & Brothers, 1917). Used by permission.

Every effort has been made to secure complete rights and permissions for each literary excerpt presented herein. Updated acknowledgments will appear in subsequent printings.

220

Book Design: Christine Ronan and Sean O'Neill, Ronan Design Chicago

Photographs: Unless otherwise noted below, all photographs are the copyrighted work of Mel Hill.

Front and Back Cover: © Alan Kearney/Viesti Collection

9 © Corbis-Bettmann

23 © Sean Kernan/Photonica

39 © Gary Benson/Tony Stone Images

55 © Stephen Wallis/Photonica

69 © John Lawrence/Tony Stone Images

87 © Chris Rainier/Corbis

103 © Key Sanders/Tony Stone Images

117 © Jerry Davis/ibid, inc.

133 © The National Archives/Corbis

147 © Josef Koudelka/Magnum Photos

161 © Charles Krebs/Tony Stone Images

175 © Betsie Van der Meer/Tony Stone Images

187 © Neil Robinson/Tony Stone Images

203 © Brad Wilson/Photonica

Picture Research: Feldman and Associates

Glossary

alliteration, the repetition of the same consonant sound at the beginning of words.

assonance, the repetition of vowel sounds across syllables or words. Assonance is a characteristic of POETRY.

audience, those people who read or hear what a writer has written.

author's perspective, a way of looking at a subject or a work of literature. An author's perspective can be influenced by background knowledge and experiences.

author's purpose, the reason why an author writes. Authors write to entertain, to inform or explain, to persuade or argue, or to express personal thoughts or feelings.

autobiography, an author's account of his or her own life.

bias, favoring (and often presenting) one side of an argument.

biography, the story of a person's life written by another person.

cause and effect, a relationship that exists when one event (the cause) brings about the other event (the effect).

characterization, the method an author uses to reveal or describe CHARACTERS and their various personalities and motives.

characters, people, animals, or imaginary creatures in a story.

connotation, the emotional meaning of a word in addition to its dictionary meaning.

consonance, the repetition of consonant sounds across syllables or words. Consonance is a characteristic of POETRY.

denotation, the exact, "dictionary" definition of a word.

description, writing that paints a colorful picture of a person, place, thing, or idea using concrete, vivid DETAILS.

details, words from a description that elaborate on subjects, characters, or action in a work. Sensory details are generally vivid, colorful, and appeal to the senses.

dialogue, the talking that goes on between CHARACTERS in a story.

drama, a GENRE or form of literature meant to be performed by actors before an audience. Drama tells its story through action and DIALOGUE. Dramas are also known as plays.

expository nonfiction, writing that explains FACTS and ideas.

fact, something that can be proven to be true.

fiction, writing that tells an imaginary story.

figurative language, language used to create a special effect or feeling. Figurative language goes beyond the literal meanings of the words used. SIMILE, METAPHOR, and PERSONIFICATION are examples of figurative language.

generalize, to take specific information and apply it to gain a broad, general insight.

genre, a category or type of literature based on its style, form, and content. The major genres are FICTION, NONFICTION, DRAMA, and POETRY.

221

highlight, to underline, circle, or mark the information that is most important as you read.

imagery, the words or phrases a writer uses to describe or present objects, feelings, actions, ideas, etc. Imagery is usually based on SENSORY LANGUAGE.

inference, a reasonable guess based upon information provided in a piece of writing.

irony (situational), the contrast between what characters or readers might reasonably expect to happen and what actually happens.

journal, a daily record of thoughts, impressions, and autobiographical information. A journal can be a source for ideas about writing.

main idea, the central point or purpose in a piece of NONFICTION.

222

metaphor, comparison of two unlike things without using a word of comparison such as *like* or *as*. Example: "The stars were diamonds."

meter, a poem's RHYTHM.

mood, the feeling(s) a story gives readers. Examples: happy, peaceful, sad.

narrative nonfiction, writing that tells a true story about people, places, or events.

narrator, the writer or speaker who tells the story or describes events in the story.

nonfiction, writing that tells a true story or explores an idea. There are many categories of nonfiction, including AUTOBIOGRAPHY, BIOGRAPHY, and essay.

objective, NONFICTION writing that relates information in an impersonal manner; without feelings or opinions.

onomatopoeia, words that sound like what they mean. Examples: buzz, crackle, hiss.

opinion, a person's personal ideas about a subject. An opinion cannot be proven true or false.

personification, a form of FIGURATIVE LANGUAGE in which an idea, object, or animal is given human characteristics. Example: "The rock stubbornly refused to move."

persuasion, writing that is meant to change the way the reader thinks or acts.

plot, the action or sequence of events in a story.

poetry, an imaginative kind of writing that tells a story, describes an experience, or reflects on an idea. It is usually characterized by STANZAS rather than paragraphs; it uses RHYTHM, FIGURATIVE LANGUAGE, SENSORY LANGUAGE, and sometimes RHYME.

point of view, the angle from which a story is told. A first-person point of view means that one of the characters is telling the story. Example: "I was angry when I left the shop, and I'm sure Leo was too." A third-person point of view means that someone outside the story is telling it. Example: "The two boys were angry when they left the shop."

predict, to use what you already know in order to guess what will happen in the future.

repetition, a figure of speech in which a word, phrase, or idea is repeated for emphasis and effect in a piece of literature.

rhyme, the similarity of sound at the end of two or more words. Rhyme is a characteristic of POETRY.

rhythm, the ordered occurrence of sound in POETRY.

satire, the use of sarcasm, humor, or exaggeration to make fun of a human vice or weakness.

sensory language, language that appeals to the five senses: sight, sound, taste, smell, and touch.

sequence, the order of events.

setting, the time and place of a story.

short story, a brief fictional narrative.

simile, a comparison of two unlike objects using *like* or *us*. Example. "The sun rose like a giant flower out of the sky."

stanza, a group of lines that are set off to form a division in POETRY.

structure, the form or organization a writer uses for a literary work. There are a large number of possible forms, such as fable, parable, romance, satire, etc.

style, how an author uses words, phrases, and sentences to form his or her ideas.

summarize, to restate briefly the most important parts of a piece of writing in your own words.

symbol, an object, person, or event that stands for something else.

theme, the statement about life or human nature that an author wants to make to the reader.

thesis statement, the summary of the author's position or VIEWPOINT in a written argument.

tone, the writer's attitude toward a subject. A writer's tone can be serious, sarcastic, objective, etc.

viewpoint, an author's opinion on a particular subject.

visualize, to see or picture in your mind what you read.

224